MW00974788

WAVES
FOR
TEENAGE
WORKFORCE
SUCCESS

How to RECRUIT, EDUCATE,
MOTIVATE, HIRE and RETAIN the
Best of Today's Teens and Young Adults

KEN WHITING

WAVES for TEENAGE WORKFORCE SUCCESS

How to RECRUIT, EDUCATE, MOTIVATE, HIRE
and RETAIN the Best of Today's Teens and Young Adults

Copyright © 2010 by Ken Whiting

Second Edition

All rights reserved. No part of this book may be reproduced or transmitted in any form or by any means, electronic or mechanical, including photocopying, recording or by any information storage and retrieval system without written permission from the publisher, except for the inclusion of quotations in a review.

Published by:
WFS Publishing
Santa Cruz, CA
www.wavesforsuccess.com

Cover design and interior layout: www.TheBookProducer.com

Printed in the United States of America

ISBN: 978-0-9815272-1-5

Dedication

To Our Crew…

Over the last couple of years as I've worked with many organizations to improve workplace productivity, it has become increasingly apparent that being an employer has provided me a unique perspective and created opportunities that otherwise would not have come my way. To the thousands of you that have chosen to work for my family's business… thank you!

To My Dad…

55 years ago you pursued a dream and took a risk to start a family business. That decision taught all of your eight children personal responsibility, strong work ethics and leadership skills at an early age. Through what you started, I was provided the professional and volunteer opportunities, which has led to the ability to write this book about the thousands of teens we have employed. You created a legacy that will carry on for generations.

Acknowledgments

While my name may be listed as the author, this is truly a team effort. Much gratitude to all.

I am blessed with a phenomenal family. My awesome wife Renee continuously provided a positive attitude, unwavering support, faith and flexibility.

My three daughters, Kendyll, Jamie and Jenny have always been my number one fans. They have taught me more about teens than anyone. As a UCLA English major, Jenny provided regular editing contributions.

I have the wonderful good fortune of having as business partners my brother and sister. Ron and Margie have fully supported me and have provided accountability and tremendous encouragement. The insights, ideas and outcomes of this book are ours.

My management team of Dan Whiting, Joanne Toth, Meaghan Campbell, Nik Whiting, Rob Holmberg and Susan Woodward either provided editing assistance, content contribution, or through their professional performance, my time was freed up for this project.

Jeff Whiting who is general manager of WAVES for Success coordinated all elements of book production and kept me on task.

Allison Nowak utilized her educational expertise and provided timely editing.

There are too many to mention, but to all my friends who are employers of teens, thank you for your willingness to share your successes, challenges and suggestions. Your friendship and expertise has been invaluable.

To the thousands of teenagers we have employed. Thanks for spending time with us. You have a choice of where you work and we appreciate that you chose our company.

My greatest gratitude goes to Almighty God. All glory and honor are His.

The best is yet to come!

Contents

The Journey Continues
2ⁿᵈ Edition Comments

It's been over two years since the original *WAVES for Teenage Workforce Success* book was published. In that period, I have had a multitude of opportunities to work with and learn more about how teens and young adults approach the workplace and what motivates them to contribute once they are there.

The slowdown of our nations economy has made jobs a hot commodity. Young folks once had their choice of where and when they chose to work because help wanted signs were everywhere and jobs were plentiful. In a very short period, the unemployment rate for students has skyrocketed to staggering levels, and competition for the fewer available positions has increased from an older workforce.

Many would think that this challenging labor market would be enough to improve their performance, and at the same time instill some good old-fashioned work ethics into an age group that had grown up often unaware of what that was. But on-the-job performance has not automatically gotten any better.

There are exceptions, and many teens and young adults that have jobs tend to be more "employer aware" when it comes to what is expected of them. There is definitely an under-standing that if they want to keep the job that they have, they had better be responsive to expectations at work. However, this generally yields forced, short-term improvements, and not the education or understanding of how and why, they should sustain that level of commitment. That is what's been missing all along. I continue to believe that without a rejuvenated management approach, employers will continue to experience a limit on their potential.

In a very recent survey I conducted of over fifty businesses that represented over ten thousand employees, not one indicated that a tougher job market created employees that were more prepared, or had improved performance.

An additional significant change that has occurred is the full adoption of social networking, and the dominant position that Facebook has garnered. Soon to have one billion members, Facebook was a distant second, with a fraction of it's current user base when we launched our original book. It cannot be ignored as a place to communicate and engage with your employees.

Through speaking engagements, consulting, convention participation, webinars and customer feedback, over the last thirty months, I have communicated with thousands of employers.

What have I learned? First of all, it's been rewarding to have everything that we originally published validated as being right on. Most employers are frustrated and challenged in getting their young workforce to consistently contribute, and we were able to provide solutions that worked.

The interaction I have had with these employers, exposed me to many additional successes. Where applicable I have weaved those improved strategies throughout this edition.

Our company continues to employ hundreds in this age group annually. I see first hand the ongoing changes in the workplace, and we are able to implement our own ideas and to develop others, that are all designed to improve their productivity and performance. It's been a positive experience and I'm able to share those results.

Much of this book is the same as the original version, in fact all of that content is still intact. This is due to the very simple reason that it works, and has stood the test of time.

On the following pages, you will find over one hundred new or expanded solutions and insights that will provide you with additional options as you continue to recruit, educate, motivate, hire and retain today's teens and young adults. And I have added an entire new chapter on the topic of how to hire the best.

While my focus continues to be on a high school and college age employee base, I hear often that the same elements that motivate and inspire a young employee are just as pertinent and effective on those that were teens many years ago. It seems we are all impacted by today's culture, communications, technology and the digital world we live in. Being a teen is just the starting point.

At WAVES For Success, our purpose has always been to educate employers on why today's teens and young adults require a new management approach, and to provide solutions, strategies and successes that will motivate, engage and inspire this age group to deliver exceptional performance.

This book is the continuation of that mission and purpose.

The journey continues.

Introduction
Why I wrote this book

Even though it was over twenty years ago, I vividly remember walking into the hotel meeting room in Atlanta, GA on the first day of the *Amusement/Theme Park Food Directors Workshop*. While honored to be included in this invitation-only event, I didn't know the other attendees. What I did know is that they must all be smarter than me! I was the new guy and they were veterans. Executives from Knott's Berry Farm, Universal Studios, King's Island, Cedar Point, San Diego Zoo, Six Flags and other attractions from around the country were represented. All of them were seasoned professionals and pillars of the industry. Everyone publicly shared and exchanged information freely. I quietly sat in the corner praying, "Please don't ask me anything." I was hoping that the next few days would pass quickly, no one would notice me, and I could just go back home.

Allow me to fast forward. Those industry leaders reached out to this new kid, asked for input, and genuinely seemed to care. They became lifetime friends, mentors and sounding boards. The value of what I've learned from them is immeasurable.

Through what these "strangers" modeled, I was inspired to engage myself in industry participation and volunteering. I get involved. I believe that you always get more than you can ever give, and I've learned so much from so many others. For thirty years, I've contributed a lot of time to community, industry and church organizations, and in every instance have been humbled by what I've gained.

These experiences are at the core of how this book came to be written. Over the years I have accumulated a wealth of business experience and an abundance of business friends from around the globe. We all have similarities in business challenges and continue to freely share experiences, expertise and solutions.

Through volunteering I've had the opportunity of giving many presentations on a variety of industry relevant topics. It was in presenting *"How to Recruit, Retain and Train a Teenage Workforce,"* an educational session I had put together for the *International Association of Amusement Parks and Attractions* annual convention in the fall of 2002, that generated the idea of this book.

Significant research went into the subject matter as it was a hot button item for the industry. I spoke with managers from dozens of companies that all shared their stories. Many had horror stories of their current experiences in recruiting and motivating a teenage workforce.

These companies recalled being frustrated, confused, let down, understaffed, and having their workforce quality lessened. Staffing shortages caused training to be significantly less, or as I heard in one instance, "non-existent." Employees were being "thrown to the wolves." The workforce reduction not only created a decrease in customer service and compromised quality standards, but also affected the workplace environment and performance of their supervisory and management staff who were now overworked. These were not the best of times.

Amusement parks are one of the most teenage-intensive businesses in the country. The experience these venues have is vast when it comes to teen employment issues. They've successfully hired, trained and dealt with the nuances of teen employees for years.

The remarks that were made at my presentation gave me two quick observations:

1. I didn't feel as bad about teen employee challenges within my business.
2. Something was changing, or had changed, in how teens were engaging in the workplace.

And if I didn't already believe that the winds of change were blowing, I found myself in a full on hurricane during and after presenting the topic. Of the hundreds of businesses represented, everyone had their own story and tried to make sure that others knew that their situation was the worst, believing that no one else could have had it as bad as they did! It became a group therapy session where managers of teens could lament about their situation and receive encouragement and hope that tomorrow was going to be a better day.

I've given the presentation dozens of times since then to different groups that were similar in the fact that they all hired teenagers. Each time, I have included updated information and revisions, gleaned from continued research, experience and feedback.

In the stories I heard there were plenty of successes and superstars. Individual efforts and small changes to process and procedures have shown to yield positive improvements. There were the occasional teens that came to the job ready and prepared for the workplace. "If only I could clone them" was a constant refrain. However, through my eyes we had reached a tipping point. What once was the norm had now become the exception, and it didn't matter if an employer had two teen employees or two thousand… it was a problem!

With every presentation I was encouraged by positive feedback and reinforcement that the information I was providing had tremendous value. People were leaving my workshops with practical new ideas and ways of looking at their situation in a new light that could generate better performance. There was always at least one person who would say, "You should write a book."

I also want to add that I have first-hand experience in the field of working with teenagers. I manage my family's business, where we annually hire hundreds of teens, equating to thousands during my thirty year career. The business started in 1953 by my father and grandfather, so I've spent quite literally a lifetime working with this age group. I never intended to become an industry expert, but in retrospect I can tell you that this first-hand experience has put me in the unique position of being able to relate to and understand much more clearly what I was hearing from others. If even on a relative basis, our experience with our teens mirrored that of others.

For years, when I was asked what I like the best and least about my job, my answer has always been the same;

> The best… Working with the teenage employees
> The least… Working with the teenage employees

It's what I know and it's what I've done. As our traditional approach gave way to change, it gave me direct access to the teen workforce that was necessary for creating the "*WAVES for Teenage Workforce Success*" system of employee management. Implementing WAVES into our program brought about positive results that were beyond our expectations.

I've been encouraged and supported the most by my family (at home), my family (at work) and a tremendous management team. Whether it's been my wife and daughters, my business partners, who are also my brother, sister and nephews, or our staff, they all routinely want to know what they can do to facilitate the process. They've given me the time and freedom to pursue this endeavor. My experience has truly been a family affair.

On a personal level, my wife and I have raised three awesome daughters and have over 30 nieces and nephews. The majority of them are now already past their teen years and most have worked in our family business. I'm pleased to say they have all successfully navigated their teen years and have thus taught me a lot. Many have provided comments on this book. I'm proud of all of them!

If not us, then who?
If not now, then when?

If you manage, supervise, hire, schedule or are in any other way impacted by a teenage workforce, then this book is written for you. I hope to not only help you improve your bottom line, but also improve your community's bottom line by your investment in the lives of the teens you can influence. I'm an advocate for elevating the role of employers in the lives of their teen employees. If not us, then who? If not now, then when?

In this book I've included experiences from our business, what we've learned about today's teens, how we came to develop the WAVES method of teenage workforce success, specific solutions that we utilized, innovative strategies from others and additional insights worthy of consideration.

This is not a book of teenage labor laws. You need to learn those and follow them, and you don't want to be surprised. The maze of rules and regulations varies by state and local municipalities. You need to be an expert, and operate within the legal framework.

If you are looking to improve how your organization functions with a teenage staff then you came to the right place. You will pick up ideas that you can immediately put to use, as well as concepts you can massage into your unique circumstances.

There is definitely not a "one size fits all" resolve to this issue. Individual dynamics of local economics, competition, population, location, budgets and other factors demand that you configure a program that will work for your business and the people you employ.

I look forward to hearing your comments, feedback, ideas and successes. Please feel welcome to email me at ken@ wavesforsuccess.com.

CHAPTER 1

The Story on Our Experience with Teenage Employees

It was the spring of 2000 and we were once again well into our hiring season. A robust economy, low unemployment rates and abundant jobs had made the prior several years by far the most challenging that our company had faced in its nearly 50 year history. This year didn't look like it was going to be any different.

We operate foodservice at the Santa Cruz Beach Boardwalk, a classic traditional amusement park with a seaside location on the Monterey Bay in California. The Boardwalk attracts large crowds for a day of fun in the sun, enjoying rides, attractions, indulgence foods and the California beach lifestyle.

Large crowds and food is where we come in, which requires a large seasonal workforce. We employ around 300 high school and college students each year. The management of our crew is always our top priority and greatest challenge.

We have always prided ourselves on the commitment we have made to our crew. We treat them like family by honoring their personal commitments, school priorities, sports, family needs and special requests. We contribute to activities and organizations that they benefit from, particularly if a current crew member is asking.

So there we were, once again, like the 3-4 prior years, facing another year with a low applicant pool and decreased availability of our current crew resulting in no selection process, being understaffed, and operating with open shifts. Not a fun place to be.

So many of the quality standards that we believed in and held up as fundamental truths in our company were challenged and compromised;

- Customer service
- Food quality
- Cleanliness
- Teamwork
- Workplace Safety

Some employees that were promoted weren't ready for the additional responsibility and we often employed volunteer groups that ended up receiving, in effect, no training.

We relied on our best employees, asking them to participate at levels that far exceeded their expectations. This caused many of them to leave for less stressful jobs.

The only satisfaction we received was from listening to stories from others around the country that employed teens and that the situation they faced may have been worse than ours. Misery loves company!

The easy answer and common refrain was that "it's the economy" and "there are more jobs than people applying." While there was a factor of truth in those statements, the economy was strong, and there were plenty of available entry-level jobs, we were seeing other changes in the workforce.

Remember, we had been in business for decades and had dealt with the entry-level, first-time-job, teenage employment challenges many times. But we couldn't ignore the intuition that there was a bigger transition occurring, something much more than simply dealing with the results of low unemployment rates.

It was those tight staffing periods, though, that masked the other changes that we were experiencing, so we hung on to the optimistic belief that even though there may not be enough employees for everyone, there's enough for us. So we would continue to simply work harder at what we had done for years and it would all work out... not!

**There may not be employees for everyone...
but there's enough for us**

Working harder and caring more turned out not to be the answer. Some of the incentives that we would use for motivation in the past were falling on deaf ears with no response. Strategies that we used for recruiting were not yielding new applicants.

Plenty of conversations occurred to determine what our solutions could be, but inevitably they would turn into recaps of the changes we were seeing. Changes in:

Attitudes

There was more of an attitude that teens were checking us out. Our employees were giving us a "test drive" so they could determine if we would be blessed with their presence.

Abilities

We used to expect that even first time job seekers knew how to clean and organize, could perform rudimentary tasks, and apply basic math skills. Not always the case.

Expectations

They didn't "expect" that we'd have expectations of them, that we'd want them to uphold their commitments. Their expectation was they could pretty much do what they want, and if we inconvenienced them, they'd simply leave.

Work Ethic

Following direction, being on time, wearing a clean uniform, practicing basic people skills like making eye contact and smiling, were all new concepts.

Common Sense

The only thing common about common sense… was how uncommon it was.

Inconsistent Performance

Even our superstar employees, those who had demonstrated positive workplace attributes that we were raising up as examples, would occasionally show up for work non-responsive, non-caring, with a total memory loss of what they had been contributing.

Lack of Respect for Supervisors and Managers

There was not any *automatic* respect for our supervisory and management teams. It seemed it had to be earned first. They were much more impacted on what their peers were doing and saying.

The benchmark that ultimately opened our eyes was that we needed a new approach, which required being open minded to new ideas. Our willingness to adapt was accelerated when I started to hear what I called the "back in my day" comments regularly from our supervisors. Comments like:

Back in my day…
I took my work responsibilities seriously

Back in my day…
I could have never gotten away with
what the kids do today

Back in my day…
I wasn't so stupid. I had common sense

Back in my day...
I read and understood what was
in the employee handbook

Back in my day...
I was at work on time,
in uniform and ready to go

Back in my day...
I'd get that job done in half the time

Back in my day...
I responded when my supervisor
asked me to do something

Back in my day...
I looked up to and respected the
supervisors and managers

• •

**It was the "Back in My Day" comments
that put us on a new path**

• •

All of these comments and the others we were hearing, on the surface looked like reflections of what I was thinking about our current young staff. However this was far more revealing than a simple confirmation from our more experienced and tenured employees.

My brother, sister and I as business partners, through different work experiences, ages and strengths, always brought different perspectives to any issue we were working on, and that has always resulted in the best final decision.

However, whenever we'd hear the "back in my day" precursor we were instantly on the same page, looking at each other in disbelief. The reason? Those supervisors making these comments, all very experienced with our company, were in their early twenties, at the oldest! From our vantage point they hadn't even had a day yet, and yet they were looking at employees just a few years younger as if there was a generation between them.

We knew then that the world was moving far too fast, and that what we were seeing was not the typical generational differences that occur. The reality was that today's teens had changed… and we had not.

. . . .

We knew then that the world was moving far too fast

. . . .

We knew that we needed to change something. We were totally committed to our crew yet we knew that leaving the status quo was not an option. We were searching for a different strategy. An approach that would be fresh and effective. Our objectives were clear. We needed to improve our:

Recruiting
Retaining
Motivation
Workplace Environment
Customer Service

If we could measure improvements in these areas, there was no doubt that growth in sales and profits would follow.

In the name of change we knew that an objective review of our operation and current procedures would be an asset. Having a qualified third party validation of what we believed was occurring would create a strong foundation for us to build from.

We were fortunate to be able to partner with *Impact Consulting*, a group of seasoned young professionals, familiar with our operation, that were closer in age to our employee demographic than they were to me. That was important! *Impact Consulting* had formed as an MBA project for these individuals, and they gave it their highest priority.

They brought themselves up to speed by hearing our story, interviewing managers and supervisors, as well as many of our teen employees, and then researching "today's teens" facts regarding lifestyle, culture and environment.

Much of what we learned through our use of their research is mentioned later in this book. However, following is a bullet point recap of their findings and recommendations:

- Identified the different and changing values, beliefs and work ethics that today's teens have.
- Determined what attitudes and behaviors we (ALL managers and supervisors) must adopt to connect with this age group.
- To improve recruiting we needed to adventure where prospective employees hang out, including the Internet.
- We needed to be a part of the high school curriculum, volunteering on campus and building allies with students, teachers and administrators.

- We needed to streamline our hiring process.
- One of their key confirmations was that work experience is low on the list of priorities of a teenager.
- All current policies needed to be examined and challenged, and obsolete policies removed. Leaving a policy simply because "we have always done it that way" could easily do more harm than good.
- They also confirmed that we were doing some things right. Our internal recruiting program, involvement in extracurricular activities, and slightly above market pay rates were successful and could be improved on for growth.

We were now in the position where we could make some nominal adjustments, or based on the information that was provided by *Impact Consulting* we could totally revamp our hiring, training and retention programs.

The cost of turnover exceeded $3,000 per person.

While still slightly undecided, I read the following recap of a study sponsored by the Coca-Cola Retailing Research Council: "The estimated total direct and indirect cost of replacing a cashier earning $6.50 per hour exceeded $3,000."

Wow... we *needed* to make fundamental changes and get total company buy-in and commitment to ensure a successful transition. I was beginning to see it as a long term necessity for sustained profitability.

So for us the journey was just beginning. Let me first go through what we had learned about today's teens and how it began to shape our next steps.

CHAPTER 2

Who Are Today's Teens?
And how it impacts their performance at work

• •

"When I was a boy of fourteen,
my father was so ignorant I could hardly
stand to have the old man around. But when
I got to be twenty-one, I was astonished
at how much he had learned in seven years."

Mark Twain

• •

Mr. Twain definitely articulated a timeless truth; the truth that every generation thinks higher of their own performance when they were teens. How soon we all forget. I certainly got that from my father, as he did from his. If you ask my kids, I've probably carried on this tradition. They actually believe my stories of walking five miles to school, barefoot in the snow, while living on the beach in Santa Cruz, California.

These ongoing generational differences are not what we are experiencing today. The world is moving faster than in any prior period in history. We are effected by the environment we are raised in, and there is no doubt that today's teens have absorbed more in their short lives than can be imagined.

This fact must be embraced, or you are headed to a continuous cycle of frustration. You'll continue attempting to make the round peg fit in the square hole. It simply won't work. If anyone in your organization is allowed to fall back into the "back in my day" syndrome, comparing your teen staff of today to when they were teens, you will never make any meaningful progress.

> **If anyone in your organization is allowed to fall back into the "back in my day" syndrome, comparing your teen staff of today to when they were teens, you will never make any meaningful progress.**

In the prior chapter, I painted the situation we faced as being dire. The fact is that there are still many great young employees who are prepared for the workforce, but what my experience and comments from others taught me is that there are a lot less of them. Today's teens are not less capable, they are simply less prepared for the work place. We had a growing number of managers scratching their heads in amazement.

I don't blame teens, and I don't believe for a second that this evolution is part of a mass conspiracy against employers. They are simply being themselves, responding to all situations from the perspective and environment of the world they have been raised in.

When I talk to teenagers about this perspective, their response ranges from dumfounded to indignant. They absolutely do not see this situation the same way. How could they?

**Today's teens are not less capable,
just less prepared for the work place**

Recently I visited an exhibit at a local museum on the human body and development of the brain. It spoke of how the brain develops at the rate of information coming in. I think most of us can agree that today's teens have taken in more information than we did up to the same age. There was a statement posted that read,

"In the adolescent brain the immature prefrontal cortex, the last region of the brain to develop, may be responsible for an increased desire for speed, danger, and rebellion, and an indifference to planning and priorities. These traits can be harmful and destructive, but it also makes teens unconventional, creative and daring thinkers. The world of music, film, literature, fashion, sports and technology would lack luster without teen spirit."

That says a lot about why all teenagers, throughout time, gain their reputation from adults. Today's teens have been raised on life's super technology highway, and the way they think is simply a reflection of that.

Following are my observations on how I see today's teens differing from when I was a teenager. These experiences and unique characteristics form the framework of how they respond at work.

BORN IN THE 90's

The majority of today's teens and young adults were born during the decade of the 90's. Think about that for a moment. That doesn't sound like very long ago... does it?

This is not Generation Y that you may have heard about. Members of Generation Y were first born in the late seventies. In many cases they are "old news or old timers" compared to the accelerated life of today's teens.

Today's teens have never used a rotary dial phone, experienced full service gas stations or feared communism. They have always known cell phones, ATM's, and terrorism. I watched *I Love Lucy* and they have Reality TV. Today coffee comes from Starbucks and sandwiches from Subway. For me the best meals are the ones that mom prepared in our kitchen. We were raised in totally different environments. It's no wonder we'd have different responses.

TECHNOLOGY:

When I was a teen in the early 1970's, the biggest technological advancement was replacing the 8-track tape with the audio-cassette. With the exception of being able to store more music in the same amount of space, that didn't have any life improving qualities.

From their first memories, all they have known is a world with cell phones, computers, the internet, voicemail, email, instant messaging, iPods, iphones, navigation systems, Google, MySpace, Facebook, EBay, and YouTube. Fax machines have already become archaic.

It doesn't feel like it was that long ago when we made the big decision to purchase an IBM Selectric Typewriter for our office. I thought we had made it! Every successful business had one. It had all the latest features, and the way you could back space to fix a typing error was genius, innovative and made us more productive. That became my benchmark for a technological breakthrough. Pretty tame by today's standards!

INFORMATION AND COMMUNICATION:
When I was a teenager, information came from the nightly news, newspaper, or from books. Communication was face to face, in writing or over the telephone. No one I knew had a telephone answering machine. Voicemail didn't exist. None of these were instant. I even had to use a pay phone, and certainly could not afford to call long distance!

Over the last decade all that has changed. Information and communication can flow in an instant and be custom tailored to the user's criteria.

We used to say that information is power. Not everyone had it, and if you did, it was a guaranteed pathway to success. Today information is available to everyone. The emphasis is on how you process and execute the information you have. Teens are "hard-wired" to process the maximum amount of facts, figures and news.

••••••••••••••••••••••••••••••••••

Teens are "hard-wired" to process the maximum amount of facts, figures and news.

••••••••••••••••••••••••••••••••••

Here is a breakdown of some of the components of how information and communication have changed:

INFORMATION

Internet

Access to uncensored information to developing minds is at the fingertips of our teenagers. Anything they want or need at any time. Less of a need to get answers from a trusted adult, or to slow down and research. I'm not so sure I could have handled growing up that fast. Access to instant information, on anything, is very empowering for a young person. *As employers we need to put that skill to work.*

Television

Over 20,000 hours has been watched by the time a person is 18 years old. Time in front of a screen (TV, computer, iPod) is now averaging over 6 hours per day! Our TV had three channels and two of them came in clear. I did have friends that had cable TV with almost 20 channels, but without it we read more.

Communicating with teens today is enhanced by using video.

24/7 News

I was raised with nightly evening news, delivered by trustworthy anchors from the three networks.

Any one station may have had up to one hour of news a day.

With the introduction of 24/7 news channels, today's teens have been enveloped in a never ending stream of negative information. That's what the news delivers. In part, teens have become more cynical and less instantly trusting. *Trust and loyalty need to be earned.*

Custom Tailored

You can now have email blasts, blogs and web links sent to your phone or computer automatically on any topic of interest you have.

That's amazing. The only correlation I can think of is the annual updates to our encyclopedia set.

You cannot simply post a memo on a bulletin board and expect the information to be read and retained.

COMMUNICATION

Cell Phones

No more mom and dad answering the phone for their teenagers when a friend calls. Privacy and independence becomes adopted at an early age.

Email

There is no need to sit down with patience, and thoughtfully write a letter.

Instant Messaging

Staying connected with friends happens more regularly, and in an instant, with our online teens.

Texting

Texting is the number one method of communications amongst teens, used much more than email. Quick, constant, short conversations.

Social Networking

The explosion of the use of social networking over the last two years cannot be ignored. *Facebook* has become the dominant "destination" and has already exceeded 500 million members, and they expect to have one billion members by the end of 2011. Approximately 90% of those in the high school and college age group visit their Facebook site daily. A growing number of hours a day are spent in these "communities."

It might be a little hard to connect the dots between this confluence of technology and communications and its impact to the workplace. While teens are definitely more comfortable using the technology you have at work, I believe that at the minimum it has hampered interpersonal skills and relationships. While teens are very comfortable "on line," they are less adept at communicating in person. In many cases, teens have gone from a home, to a home page for community.

There is nothing wrong with technology and all that it brings into our lives. I have totally adopted the latest innovations and can barely imagine life without them. The fastest growing age group for Facebook members is forty and older. The difference is that I know the difference. My life experience evolved from manual to automatic, from simple to complicated, from slow and steady to a blur.

••••••••••••••••••••••••••••••••••

**In many cases, teens have gone from a home,
to a home page for community.**

••••••••••••••••••••••••••••••••••

CULTURE

When I was a teen, gas cost less than 50¢ a gallon, and my Volkswagen got over 30 mpg. We were always outside playing impromptu games or creating projects with neighborhood friends. Families always had dinner together, and it was a rarity to dine in a restaurant. Bottled water… what was that? At school we said the Pledge of Allegiance and it was acceptable to pray. The country watched as President Richard Nixon resigned over the Watergate scandal. The thought of a school shooting was unimaginable. Besides the basic necessities of food, clothes and a roof over my head, I was totally responsible for paying for any type of "extras." Credit cards were not an option. All of my friends had or wanted jobs, and you had to work hard to get one.

That is a brief reflection of my memory of being a teenager. They were good times, but the times have changed. There is no way that a teenager today would ever be able to relate to those years. They shouldn't have to. It doesn't matter. However, those circumstances, and whatever yours were, affects the way we view how teenagers today respond.

Take a look at some other observations about how our culture has changed:

Families

We are a long way from mom being home all day while dad went off to work… at the same company until retirement. Today, teens are just as likely to be a part of a blended family or be raised by a single parent. This and other factors can result in less time together as well as adding pressures on applying and enforcing what was in my day traditional discipline.

In addition, there is a likelihood that one of the parents has been laid off, outsourced, or victimized by the dot com bust or other frailties of our economy. My parents and the parents of my friends all supported the employer and encouraged their kids to "show up, shut up and do what you are told." Today teens may not get much positive work advice at home.

Physical Fitness

There is a higher percentage of teens today that get less physical activity. More time is spent in front of a video screen, many schools have cut P.E. classes, diets have become less nutritional, and news on the obesity epidemic is common. This would certainly effect energy levels, and the quantity and intensity of work that can be accomplished.

I'm often times amazed at the comments our employees have about how tired they are or how hard they have worked. I'm not taking anything away from their contributions, but their ability for sustained physical work is less.

School

At one level, competition to enter our nations best universities is at an all time high. At the other end of the spectrum, the percentage of high school students who never graduate is also at record breaking levels. Budgets in schools have been cut requiring many extra curricular programs to be eliminated. Support positions, like work experience coordinators, are also gone, leaving a void in the quantity and quality of work readiness training. Campus safety is top of mind daily for administrators, teachers and students. Students receive less discipline, have more freedom and don't have access to as many arts programs.

Through my involvement with Rotary, I've had the pleasure and opportunity to meet many high school exchange students. One of Rotary's areas of service is through its Youth Exchange program. Locally, each school year, there are always several students from around the world being hosted by local families. These exchange students will always visit the Rotary Clubs to meet the members and to tell of their visit. When asked what are the biggest differences between their home and life in the USA, they always respond that our schools are academically easier with less classroom discipline.

High schools used to be the training grounds for students' first jobs. They came to the employer with an understanding of work ethics.

While giving a presentation recently in Salt Lake City, the daily newspaper had a front page story on the issue that 25% of the area's high school "graduates" did not pass the state exit exam. What a tragic disservice to these students, and a graphic picture of the readiness of many of our young staff. It's an oxymoron to have graduates who haven't achieved the minimum academic requirements.

It seems like much more attention has been given to self esteem than personal responsibility. Placing a higher priority on how a student feels and looks over their results does not prepare them for employment. I'm not opposed to building self-confidence, but at the end of the day it's results that matter. If a teen has been raised in a world where they've never made a mistake, where there are no losers or winners, where simply participating is winning, and trying is good enough, they will suffer at work.

Sports

Sports used to be something you did for yourself. It was for fun. It was the perfect place to build self-confidence and self esteem because you worked hard and earned it. While perhaps not for everyone, somewhere along the way it changed. Now it's not just about the teen or team. Parents have engaged themselves at curious levels. A coach's performance is always under review. Single sports must be selected and focused on all year. You've failed if you don't start, make the varsity or are headed towards a college scholarship.

When hard work and teamwork are not the goals, the wrong message is being sent.

Branded World

McDonald's has over 30,000 restaurants and Subway just a few less. Starbucks has more than 15,000 on their way to their stated goal of 40,000. Walk through any mall and you will pass one retail chain after another. Independent grocery stores are few and far between. Product advertising of soft drinks, alcohol, music, electronics, clothing and entertainment has all become very strategic, teen focused and omnipresent in their lives.

What does this mean? The delivery of messages designed to be heard, memorable and create a call to action, are strategic, scientific, specific and systematic. If you have an important message to communicate, you'll need to employ the same look, feel, and processes that are used to market products to teens.

Consumer Driven Society

Every generation wants more "stuff." A difference that I see today is that through media's arms, there is intensive pressure constantly communicating new benefits and must-have features. This flow can become overwhelming. With the inclusion of being able to buy now and pay later through credit cards, the massive consumption of consumer goods that exists today has been fueled.

Less value is placed on quality and decisions are impulsive. Teens bring this short-term approach to work.

Entertainment

I went to movies, a few concerts, school sporting events, and hung out at the amusement park. Not much different from how today's teens fill their time. One addition to the entertainment mix, though, has been the growing participation and impact of video games. It has become a multi-billion dollar industry that continues to outpace other entertainment options. Honestly, I don't have a first hand exposure to the latest versions of these computer games. I did own Pong when it came out but that was pretty much my first and last foray.

Video games are becoming more controversial. Many teens are spending on average up to two hours per day playing games that are becoming more compelling, life-like and violent. Not all video games are bad. There are many games with an educational focus and content that can serve a positive purpose. However, violence has become a theme to the most popular games, and the interactive and graphic qualities can begin to numb the senses to reality.

Read a portion of a study conducted by Gentile, Lynch, Linder & Walsh in 2004:

"adolescent girls played video games for an average of 5 hours a week whereas boys averaged 13 hours a week." The authors also stated that teens who play violent video games for extended periods of time show the following behaviors:

1. *Tend to be more aggressive*

2. *Are more prone to confrontation with their teachers*

3. *May engage in fights with their peers*

4. *See a decline in school achievements.*
   (Gentile et al, 2004).

Another negative impact is that players are rewarded for their violent acts. The interactive quality of video games differs from passively viewing television or movies because it allows players to become active participants in the game's script. Players benefit from engaging in acts of violence and are then able to move to the game's next level.

Habits are created and personalities adjusted while playing these games. This could lend itself to some teen employees being unable to exist with their coworkers and within the confines of the rules and procedures at work.

APPEARANCE:

Self expression and personal appearance has always been high priority for teens. Tattoos, body piercing and hair styles/colors are not acts of rebellion. Carving out their individuality is a natural response to the bombardment of messages they receive on how to look and act. Teens are inundated with pictures of perfect success, success that generally is impossible to attain.

Don't pass judgment based on appearance. As a rule it is not a reflection on what their performance will be. It also doesn't mean that they need to be hired. Their "brand" may not be consistent with, or in the best interest of your "brand." Uniform and grooming policies need to be evaluated, perhaps adjusted, established, communicated, purpose explained and consistently enforced.

ROLE MODELS:

Maybe I am getting older. I believe teens would be well served by positive adult influences in their lives. People like parents, pastors, teachers, coaches and employers. But what I see are more teens modeling the dress, style and attitudes of a different kind of role model. The new standard is set to be instant millionaires, celebrity athletes, movie stars and recording artists. A common denominator is money and the lifestyle that it can bring. I would guess this is made popular through the sheer amount of media influence.

I believe this can bring out the unintended consequence of setting teens up for failure, while creating a double-edged sword. On one side teens may exhibit disillusionment in an entry level job, believing that it won't get them to their dreams. Why should they work hard? In their mind they are just passing time until they hit it big. On the other side this is an opportunity for employers to become more engaged and to be a positive influence in the lives of their teenage employees.

SPEED IS EVERYTHING

Teens are definitely raised in a 24/7, got-to-have-it-now world. From main street to the internet, in their lifetime, we never close for business. When I was a teen, most businesses were closed in the evenings and on Sundays. My generation was happy to let our fingers do the walking. Today you just "Google it."

I remember when the movie the *Wizard of Oz* was on TV. It was an annual event that we anticipated and planned our day around. The entire family gathered around to enjoy a couple of hours together. How odd that must seem to today's teens who can instantly download any movie they want to their iPods for individual viewing.

Thought and acquisition can occur at the same time. Competition for mindshare is intense, and quantity of decisions to be made is endless. Don't expect to witness patience as a virtue at work.

· ·

Don't expect to witness patience as a virtue at work

· ·

My guess is that you'll analyze these observations based on your age. The older you are, the more you'll be agreeing, and adding your own observations to the list. The younger you are, you may be disagreeing or viewing these as criticisms, which they are not.

By the way, I'm not opposed to today's culture and technological advances. I can't imagine my life without them. To not have an interest, or at least a curiosity about technological advances would be the equivalent of still riding a horse and buggy. I like my car!

Life today is not wrong. All technology and cultural changes aren't right. But it is the way it is.

As an influencer of teens, you need to look at your teen employees not through the eyes of when you were their age but through their eyes. Understand their circumstances, priorities and environment they have been raised in.

I mentioned earlier that I believe teens today are as capable as they have ever been. Maybe more so. They are just less prepared for the workplace. Who is giving them workplace education and training? Who is preparing them to enter a business and have a rudimentary idea of what their contribution and expectation ought to be? A few years ago I was presenting a seminar and included a piece I had picked up on comments that Bill Gates had made to a high school graduation class. He had ten rules for success. It was a straight forward, work hard, pay your dues and honor your parents type of advice. As a major surprise to me, it was by far what I received the most comments about and requests for. That audience was convinced it was what their teen staff hadn't heard! You'll find those quotes in the resource section at the back of this book.

There is one other overriding theme that I see coming up often. It's the pace of this change with technology and in our culture.

I speak with many young managers. Individuals that are on one side or the other of twenty-five years old. Without fail, in every case, they will begin to give me their "back in my day stories," just like I was receiving from my supervisors a few years ago. They look at their employees in the 15 – 20 year age range as a younger generation. They can't believe how much has changed so quickly.

Think about this. I mentioned Facebook a little earlier. The Facebook platform launched in January 2004 and is approaching its 7th anniversary as a company. In that time-frame their growth is incomparable to anything else, and it was highly driven on the full adoption by the age group we are discussing. Facebook is on a fast track to one billion members!

Today's teens have been raised in a world far different than mine, and probably yours too.

The future is coming and employers better be ready.

Teens can be inspired to excel at work, and contribute to your business success. Let's talk about that!

CHAPTER 3

Teens CAN Be Inspired and Self Motivated

In many ways these young people were far more accomplished than their predecessors. Their achievements in sports, academics, volunteering, music, arts, drama and technology far exceed anything from my teen years.

It had evolved into a good news/bad news situation.

• •

They performed better away from work

• •

The bad news was that their job was simply a means to an end. They needed to earn a little extra money, their parents said they had to have a part time job, or it was something to do in the summer between school years. There was a disconnect between their workplace responsibilities and expectations, with their life priorities, hobbies and other interests. They performed better away from work.

The good news was that along with often confounding us, they were demonstrating amazing positive qualities. They were raised in an environment that may not have put an emphasis on practical entry level work skills, however these teens are well prepared to take on the world they will soon lead.

A key point from the last chapter is that teens are capable, just less prepared for the workplace. I firmly believed that the quality, capabilities and integrity of our teenage crew hadn't changed, however their readiness for the workforce certainly had. They processed the significance of a job in a far more casual manner and didn't automatically respond to authority.

I was determined to figure out how we could get our crew to be motivated at work.

Our first step was to simply ask our teenage employees what they thought about our company, supervision and the work they had to perform. The answers simply raised more questions. Everything was great they said. They loved working for us. They were treated well, liked their coworkers and supervisors, and didn't complain about the pay scale or the duties they had to perform. That should have been a recipe for success.

In conversations with our teen staff I was amazed at the stories I was hearing of their commitment to what they were passionate about. They were taking preparedness classes and extra study sessions for the SAT tests so that they would be accepted into major universities. They were participating year round in sports, both on school teams and more competitive regional club teams.

This dialogue yielded insight into the fact they could understand complex topics associated with technology. They understood how things worked, and often were able to program or repair the technology they used. To my surprise, many volunteered for their favorite school, church or social cause, and were articulate about the mission and purpose. If they were involved in an activity, they were fully engaged.

Our employees spoke proudly of their willingness to listen, learn and respect those that guided their extra curricular paths. Coaches, teachers, advisors, older friends and mentors were held in high esteem. No doubt that if they were asked to come early, stay late, wear a certain uniform or abide by some other team, class, or group policy, they would do it.

> *Teens can be motivated to do what they WANT, not just what they NEED to do.*

Who were these people? This is not what we were seeing exhibited. They were demonstrating the skills and responsibilities that we required, however they just weren't using them at work. Teens can be motivated to do what they WANT, not what they NEED to do.

It's clear that being raised in today's environment is far different from my days of being a teenager. Less personal responsibility and real world common sense has been surpassed by other character skill sets, that I only wish I had at the same age. A few strengths of today's teens are:

Adaptable
This is an age group that embraces change and will adjust to any new reality that you present

Committed
While it won't come automatically, if you earn their respect, they will be loyal and totally committed

Innovative
They will look for ways to improve your products, processes and procedures

Knowledgeable & Skilled
Better informed than any teenage group from the past

Multi-Taskers
While in some cases they may have traded quality for quantity, they are capable of doing more than one thing at a time

Resilient
Challenges of the business day won't rock their world

Time Efficient
Willing to use technology to make the most of their time

Tolerant
Raised in a multi-cultural world, they have a willingness to work with everyone

Still a question begged. If they were self motivated and constructive in other activities, how do we get that result at work? In fact they were so self motivated, they'd routinely and without a conscience put those priorities in front of any work commitment they had made. It would not be unusual for them to respond in the following ways if work conflicted with whatever else they had going on;

- Call in sick (when they weren't)
- Submit last minute time off requests
- Not show up for their shift
- Quit their job

What we were seeing in their personal lives didn't match up to what they were delivering at work. There really was a disconnect. They were demonstrating that they did have a work ethic and could respond to direction. They understood responsibility, discipline and teamwork.

Now What?

How could we create a workplace that would self motivate our teen staff to utilize their abilities and interests?

Since we were seeing them excelling in their hobbies, we knew they were able to do the same at work. Not looking to reinvent the wheel, it made sense to attempt to model after these same activities.

Following is an outline of the exercise we went through as we began to adapt:

1. Identified the long time activities in our area that are sustained by teenagers

2. Identified the positive attributes of those activities that are transferable to the workplace

3. Identified those employees or other teens that we had access to who participate in those activities, and involve them in the process

In Texas it might be high school football. Los Angeles drama and theatre clubs. In New York City music and bands might prevail while in the Midwest, the rodeo. There's no magic to this, or right or wrong answers. Find out how teenagers choose to spend their time in a positive environment. I'm not talking about hanging out at the mall, but activities that have them fully engaged, involved with others, and where a goal of personal improvement exists.

It may be obvious, or you may have to do a little research, but it won't be hard to identify multiple choices.

That's what we did.

The final choice for us was simple. Santa Cruz, California is the quintessential beach town, where countless teens have grown up riding waves.

Your first thought might be "surfing?" Your only exposure may be watching the character Spicoli in the movie *Fast Times at Ridgemont High*. Spicoli exemplified the "hey dude," "totally awesome," longhaired stoner, unintelligent stereotype that some may have of surfing. But that picture is a long way from the truth.

In any activity you can find the fringe, non-committed that aren't participating for personal development and growth. That would be true in surfing, and Spicoli played that role well. You are looking for positive characteristics. Just leave the negative stuff behind.

Plenty of our crew were surfers. In the past we never thought of finding out what we could learn from them. We figured we had learned enough. When the waves were breaking, they called in sick! We couldn't afford to learn anymore. But it was a new day that required a fresh approach, and for the length of my thirty year career, surfing has been a staple part of the landscape, kept alive by the infusion of a continual inflow of teens.

We developed a list of questions that we believed would provide insightful answers.

The questions we asked were;

Who do you surf with?
What do you like about surfing?
When is your favorite time to surf?
Where do you usually surf?
Why do you enjoy surfing?
How did you first learn and continue to learn to improve in surfing?

There was one follow up question to all of the above:
Why is that important?

Answers to these questions were revealing, and included:

Challenge
They sought after the challenge of riding bigger, faster waves and were prepared to do what it took to be ready

Desire to Improve
*They sincerely wanted to be better surfers
than they were currently*

Discipline
*They were committed to consistently doing
what it took to reach their goals. If it meant
being in 55 degree water every morning before
school to practice, they would do it*

Dress Code
*Surfing has a "look," and the style of clothes,
bleached hair and suntanned skin are freely
embraced as the uniform of choice*

Enthusiasm
They spoke with excitement about the surf culture

Equipment
*They understood the specific uses of different types
of surf boards, leashes, wetsuits and their impact on
wave size, winds, tides and temperatures*

Goals
*They were determined to achieve the goals
they had of the size of wave, or surf break
location they wanted to reach*

History
*They had an appreciation of the lore and history
of the sport and for the "old guys" who were
legends on the same waves they surfed*

Image
Surfing is a visual sport that is brought to life through magazines, movies and music. They fully embrace the surf image

Independence
When you are paddling into a wave, it's up to you and only you, on whether you succeed or wipe out. You learn to make your own decisions

Instant Gratification
Immediately after the work of paddling out and into a wave, the reward is the ride. This instant gratification drives them to do it again

Opportunity
Just like those in more traditional sports dream of playing in the NFL, NBA or MLB, our teenage surfers spoke of careers as professional surfers or working with a company that serves the industry

Positive Attitude
I never heard that they couldn't be successful. They spoke with a positive, can-do attitude

Respect
They had a strong respect for the dangers, the power of waves and precautions for their safety

Slang/Language
Surfing has a use of nicknames, nomenclature and slang that connects them to the sport and to others they surfed with

Willingness to Be Taught
They are open to learning from older more experienced surfers

Willingness to Help Others
They want to train and give advice to others

That exercise provided the final piece of evidence that teens were more than capable to excel at work. It was up to us as an employer to make necessary adjustments to leverage their contributions.

This is not about hiring surfers. Non-surfer employees can be equally influenced by what we learned. This is about you learning from your employees and seeing life through their eyes. I'm certain that no matter where they invest their time, answers will be similar to ours.

I should note there will always be employees who don't seem to care or aspire very high. They may be average students at best and not overly involved in extra curricular activities. We had employees who didn't like their job and honestly under different hiring environments should have never been employed.

. . . .

It's only through focusing on what *can* happen that real change occurs.

. . . .

Besides it being my personal nature, emphasis on only positive characteristics is purposeful. Only through focusing on what can happen does real change occur.

Acknowledge that not all of your teen staff will be overachieving superstars. Grow your base of employees who can and want to contribute at work. There are teens that simply don't have the maturity to hold a job. While I'm an advocate of providing second, third and often fourth chances to a young employee, you are running a business and there must be limits. You can only do so much. There's a time to make those employees who simply aren't ready for the workplace your competitor's challenge. Besides being the right thing to do, it will go a long way into building loyalty from the rest of your staff.

● ●

Teens had changed, and we hadn't.

● ●

Teens had changed, and we hadn't. While the above outlined our approach to learning how to inspire and tap into this age group at work, following is a synthesized list of what countless employers have shared with me regarding how to motivate teenagers.

Clear Goals: Don't let them operate in a vacuum. Set goals, outline the framework and provide feedback.

Incentives: This is a "what's in it for me" generation. Provide a cause an effect between their efforts and what they receive. By the way, incentives do not have to be high priced items that you view as an expense. Win-win scenarios are easily created.

Friends: Teens have always been influenced by their friends and peers. We have built many solutions into our WAVES solutions on how to leverage this.

Participation: Ask for their ideas and feedback. You can build loyalty by including them in the process. It doesn't mean you have to act on their suggestions. By soliciting comments and ideas you are valuing them, and that will raise their performance.

Communication: This really is the glue that holds the other pieces together. However, it is just as important in *how* you communicate as *what* you communicate. This is a digital world, and using technology is key to being heard.

Concern, Respect & Courtesy: For many high school and college age employees, you may be the only place that is modeling these attributes. Value their contributions, be polite, show respect, listen, make eye contact and smile. Simply model the service you are asking them to provide. This human connection may be the greatest motivator of all.

. . . .

The human connection may be the greatest motivator of all.

. . . .

Recently I saw results of a research study completed by Deloitte Consulting (check this and other info out at www. deloitte.com). All of their findings support and collaborate what we learned as employers, and from employers.

In regards to how they are impacted by a personal and human connection, they found teens were likely to;

- Partner well with mentors
- Value guidance
- Expect respect
- Embrace collaboration

There are many additional findings in their study that identify the characteristics and beliefs that shape how they will perform at work.

Our purpose was lucid: Create an environment that allowed for teens to WANT to be self motivated and inspired and figure out how to transfer their life skills into work skills.

It was time to catch a WAVE.

CHAPTER 4

Catching a WAVE
A New Way to Motivate Today's Teens

This story began during the most challenging time in our business history, which was several years ago and thankfully we have seen better days. Since then we have had the unique opportunity of continuing to observe and learn from our teenage crew members. Our radar has been heightened as we are always on the lookout for successes, both our own and from others. Signs of improvement are showing up everywhere.

Besides learning from our own employee base, I continued to accept speaking engagements at a variety of industry and corporate training sessions. At every occasion I was able to brainstorm, share, and listen, as well as receive feedback, comments and suggestions for improvements on how to successfully recruit, educate, motivate and retain today's teens.

Successes were occurring, generally based on a willingness to implement new strategies that simply came from necessity. Many employers experimented with different techniques and strategies to involve their teen staff. Often times epiphanies yielded radical new approaches to employee management.

My travels around the country, constant conversations with other employers and the ingenuity of our management team was creating an extensive list of these successes.

I had accumulated quite a stockpile of innovative and proven best practices, evolutions of current programs, theories, and ideas based on what we had learned about today's teens.

The combined impact of these successes provided encouragement that with an open mind to change, we could not just succeed, but excel in the area of managing our young employee base.

I categorized these ideas under one of these premises;

- The teen lifestyle and culture needed to be integrated into the workplace environment.

- Teens today are opinionated, independent and knowledgeable. How do we use that at work?

- The way teens learn and retain information and communicate has changed. We needed more video and digital content, and less paper.

- Someone needed to provide teens with the basic workplace ethics, responsibility, and the value of a job message. What was once the domain of parents, teachers and counselors has now been left for employers.

- How teens look and how they are treated are more important today than ever. More significantly, how they respond to these issues has really changed.

With our own improvements becoming more regular and insightful, I continued to share these concepts with others. Both in formal presentations and casual conversation the feedback I received was positive.

* * * * *

WAVES for Success was born

WAVES for Teenage Workforce Success was born to provide an umbrella for all teen employment, and workplace procedures and processes.

WAVES is an acronym for:

Way of Life
Attitude
Verbal, Video and Visual Communication
Education… not just Training
Style Matters

We created our own special recipe. We merged the experiences of employers, including our own, with what we learned was true of today's teens. We then blended it with what we knew teens enjoyed about their hobbies and areas of personal interest.

I hope that through the following three points, you receive compelling reasons to view your teen staff through a new lens:

Experience: Our personal experience employing hundreds of teens annually supports the fact that the same old practices just don't work any more. Collaborated now by hundreds of other employers, it's time to take a fresh look at how to motivate teens in the workplace.

Education: I outlined many of the environmental and cultural changes that have impacted how teens view life. Some are subtle and others more overt, however the combined impact, and turbulent pace, would suggest that as employers we better get on board.

Encouragement: I hope that you believe, as I do, that today's teens routinely demonstrate they can be over achievers, ambitious and have the ability to be inspired, motivated and goal oriented.

WAVES came from the connection between our teenage staff and surfing. As mentioned earlier, we received quite an education from our employees that surfed, and how to transfer those positive qualities into the workplace.

The WAVES acronym was an easy selection for us. We like how we were able to use each letter to categorize our new way of looking at teenagers at work.

The word WAVES also painted a picture of success. As an analogy it described perfectly the kinds of new strategies we designed. When surfing you need to take advantage of the power of a wave. You have to be ready <u>before</u> it gets there, <u>stay out in front</u>, and paddle <u>with</u> the wave, not against it.

This represented the kinds of solutions we want to present. Those that will have you prepared for the future, and not just one time with short term results. As new changes come at you, these are solutions that will keep you out in front.

These approaches will improve your recruiting, retention and motivation of your teenage workforce.

I should warn you that there isn't one magic idea that will solve all your challenges. Your perfect resolves may be a combination of items listed, customized to the unique circumstances of your business and the local labor and economic marketplace.

Keep looking at your workplace not through the eyes of when you were a teenager, but through the eyes of today's teens. That cloudy view will begin to clear up as you benefit from growing productivity and contribution from your teenage staff.

It's time to ride some WAVES!

CHAPTER 5

Way of Life – *Create It*
Improving the Workplace Environment

Your Teen Staff Are the Face of Your Company

The definition of "Environment" is: *"The conditions that surround people and affect the way they live."*

Think of WAY of LIFE as the workplace environment; *"The conditions that surround people and affect the way they work."*

When we interviewed many of our teen employees that surfed, one thing that clearly revealed itself was that they liked the lifestyle that came from their participation. There was a look that was attractive, people who they enjoyed, common goals, music and an atmosphere of fun that came from the surfing culture.

Appreciate the fact that young staff members are the way they are. Remember that it's not wrong, nor right, it's just the way it is. Teens need to be reached where they are at.

Set the bar high, but don't be afraid of some failure. Don't focus on what they've done wrong. Build your relationship by encouraging them on what they are doing right. They will become extremely loyal when they are taken seriously and treated with respect.

Following are ways to improve the Way of Life and workplace environment:

BE WELCOMING

The saying, "you only get one chance to make a first impression" applies here. An additional caveat though is that the "first impression" needs to repeat itself on nearly a daily basis.

On each occasion when you are seeing one of your teenage employees for the first time *that day,* reach out to them with a friendly, "good to see you... glad you're here." It may sound coddling, but for many teens who have had their lives micromanaged by parents, it is an environment that they are used to and will therefore respond to.

While this applies to one of your seasoned employees, it is especially true for your new employees. Go out of your way to make them feel like you are honestly glad that they chose you as their place of employment.

One final key point is to make sure that all of your managers or supervisors are in the habit of doing this. You should have some type of system that ensures that those in authority within your organization have met and reached out to all new teen employees. If schedules don't allow for that to occur within the first couple of weeks, a phone call to their home by the owner, senior manager or their representative would have a lasting impact.

CELEBRATE SUCCESS

When you have one of your teenage employees become employee of the month, set a new sales record, receive a perfect shopping report or a positive comment from a customer, demonstrate exceptional performance, win an employee contest, have perfect attendance, work anniversary, submit a new idea, participate in a training program, receive a promotion, or any one of dozens of other workplace accomplishments... you need to make a lot of noise about it.

More importantly when it comes to celebrating success, promote the life achievements that are being experienced away from work. Are they starring in their high school play, did their sports team go to the playoffs, did they get accepted to college, buy a new car or named king or queen of the prom? This is the important information of their life. Celebrate it by promoting it at work. Somehow, somewhere, have a place where you can post or communicate this information so that everyone who is working will see it.

Do you acknowledge their birthdays and graduations? A hand written card mailed to their home from their employer will definitely stand out.

How do you get this information? Keep your ears open and make sure supervisors have a way to communicate what they hear.

After some period of time of sharing this type of personal information, their friends, coworkers and themselves will be supplying you with all the info you'll ever need to promote the individual "non workplace" highlights of your employees. Develop a plan of how you will handle this information.

ALLOW SOME FAILURE

Every mistake ought to serve as an educational moment. Take the time to provide the insight that you have about the error that occurred. Find out what was learned. Only be concerned if the same mistake repeats itself over and over again.

* *
"Don't fire them... Fix them"
* *

There's an attraction called the Mystery Spot in Santa Cruz owned by a friend of mine. They are highly regarded for their overall level of customer service and quality.

He has a theme for his employee management: "Don't fire them... Fix them."

I'm convinced that philosophy is foundational to their success. His managers and supervisors can't take the easy way out and terminate the employment of one of their young staff members. The culture of their business demands that they invest time into the employee on additional education, training and understanding.

In addition to the "don't fire them, fix them" response to employee performance, almost automatically their hiring process improved. More time is spent on selecting job applicants that better match up to their needs.

EMPHASIZE FUN

This doesn't mean to not take work seriously, but the environment needs to be light and fun. Managers and supervisors need to know how to interact with a young staff. If there is an issue, deal with it. Otherwise have a good time and let others enjoy themselves at work.

INCLUDE MUSIC IN THE WORKPLACE

An effective way to receive an upbeat, positive attitude from your teenage employees is to get them motivated with music. You can still choose the type of music to be played. Just make sure it's relevant to the age group. Often times it isn't appropriate to have music playing in customer areas. In that case, make it available to back rooms and check in areas.

PROVIDE LIFE MENTORING

There was a time when the workplace would have been the last place that a teenage employee could have expected any life advice or direction. I'm not suggesting that an employer's role be expanded to replace the advice received from parents and teachers. However, due to a variety of circumstances, many teens do not get career and life guidance. They are left to figure life out for themselves, or through TV, movies and the Internet.

I hear all the time from employers about the unofficial expanded role they have taken on in a teen's life. Why not formalize it a little and provide educational materials or bring in speakers that promote the value of financial planning and investments, goal setting and time management, career pathways, benefits of fitness and nutrition, and continuing education. This can cost next to nothing, but will build tremendous loyalty and improved performance.

BRAND EVERY PROGRAM

Anyone born in the last 15-20 years has been raised in a branded world. From quick service restaurants, clothing, music, movies, even sermons at church, there is an image created with a defined look and feel. If you want to grab the attention of a young employee for a new program, give it a unique, easily remembered, branded look. With computers and just a hint of graphics knowledge, you can create an effective brand. And if you can't do it, in all likelihood one of your teenage employees can! The use of images and color will draw attention and retention.

Following are a couple of changes we made. Each of these programs has a graphic image that helps to make the program memorable.

- Employee of the Week, became *You're a Star.*

- Employee Suggestion program, became *I.D.E.A.S.*
  (**I**ntelligent **D**ata **E**valuated **A**nd **S**ubmitted)

- Internal Recruitment Program, became *Crew Search.*

SOCIAL EVENTS

For a young, largely entry-level workforce, the effect their friends have on them will always be more powerful than workplace responsibilities. Having fun with their peers will most always win out. This is a reality you should embrace.

Build into your budget and program at least a couple of social events a year. It doesn't have to be much because it's about being together.

If it isn't practical to get your entire staff together at one time, then do it in smaller work groups. If that doesn't work, then provide a social event for them by giving out certificates to movies or dinner that can only be enjoyed by multiple employees at the same time.

To get the maximum benefit, allow your employee to include a "non employee" friend. This will build participation and expose your company to possible future employees.

While emphasis needs to be on having these events be fun, it's a good idea to have a purpose or message attached to each event. It may be "customer service" or "product quality" night, where your teenagers need to describe their observations.

Romance Your History and Community Participation

Tell the story of how your business was founded and the role that your company plays in the local or broader community. Teens want to be a part of something bigger than themselves. Often times the legacy of your company is a story that will educate and instill pride. If you have a commitment to give to your community, then support a project your teens can support and be personally involved with.

Don't Let Them Quit

Often times when a teen quits it isn't because they are unhappy with their job. It's due to the fact that life priorities have taken precedence. School work, extra curricular activities or family commitments take priority. Those are larger issues than what is generally an entry-level, seasonal or part-time job.

Set up an "on-call" category of employees. These can be employees who you don't want to lose, but for the reasons mentioned above they can't work. By being on-call, they would never be scheduled or expected to check a schedule. But when you have a short term or emergency need, they are available to call, providing you with no loss of productivity.

Communicate with your on-call group as if they were regularly scheduled employees. Keep the connection. Attach criteria to how often they need to work or some way for them to demonstrate an ongoing interest. When their situations change, you will be the obvious choice for their job commitment.

CONNECT WITH PARENTS/FAMILIES

For younger teens, connect with their families. Send home a letter to parents introducing yourself as their child's employer. Be clear about what you expect of their child and share your commitment to work around their school and hobby schedule. Let parents know who they can check in with and the best way to reach that person.

Provide discounts and extend appropriate benefits to family members. Have a family discount day or free meal day.

CONNECT WITH SCHOOLS

Reach out to local high schools and colleges. Meet the principal and offer your services and support. Find out how you can be involved in a useful way to their student body. Provide similar benefits to staff and teachers that you make available to families. Don't forget the home school community.

INTERNAL RECRUITMENT PROGRAMS

This may serve as a model for a variety of workplace challenges. Broaden their workplace expectations and go beyond the tasks of their job. When recruiting was a challenge for our company, we made our crewmembers our recruiters. We developed a program called *Crew Search*, created business cards for them to use. We made our employees part of the solution. It worked brilliantly, as our current crew actively embraced it and recruited people in their circle of influence. We were able to cancel any other advertising we were doing and more importantly filled all of our shifts, improving customer service and sales along the way.

Consider this approach if (or when) recruiting is a challenge for you.

You will begin to see a different response from teens when you make the connection between other areas of their life and work. Bridging with their families, schools, extra curricular activities and hobbies, friends, and life success will have a positive impact on the workplace environment, and set the stage for improved contributions from teenagers.

Consider additional *Way of Life* additions. Do you have room to make a computer and the internet available for them to use before/after their work shifts? Are you set up to communicate with them by email and texting? It might not be the way you send out information, however it is the preferred way for a teen to respond.

● ●

Your teen staff are the *face* of your *company.*

● ●

Think about that. In most places where teenagers are employed they are in the most important position that a company can have; the one that is closest to the customer. Their interaction and customer service can create either a lifetime customer, or the last visit to your business.

Set them up for success. Review what you are asking of them and be clear of your expectations. What policies do you have simply because you have always had them? How welcoming are they?

It all starts with the interview. That is both the employer's and prospective employee's chance to make that first impression. Do not let them bring a way of life into *your* workplace that doesn't represent your company. And don't make promises about job benefits that you know won't occur.

With all that said about *Way of Life*, there has been much success experienced. When the paradigm shifts to treating your employees at the same or higher level of how you treat customers, and in the manner they want to be treated, you'll begin to see real progress in how your teen staff responds and performs.

CHAPTER 6

Attitude – *Feed It*

Recognition = Retention

Teenagers can have many different attitudes. Teens come with an attitude of independence and "what's in it for me." They can have a positive, can-do, "the sky is the limit" attitude. Other times they have an attitude of disinterest and are disconnected from work. And we've all experienced the generational, right of passage teenage *attitude* of "Don't bother me, I'm smarter than any adult."

No matter what attitude you experience the most, getting your programs and approach in sync with how a teen thinks will pay off in massive productivity growth and remarkable retention.

Through researching successes from others and interviewing our own teenage crew, we identified many high impact areas that will positively improve the attitudes and performance of a teenage employee.

FLEXIBLE SCHEDULES

This seems to be one of the most problematic benefits promoted by employers. Most employers understand that to fully gain support from a teenage employee, they need to allow for that same teen to participate in extra curricular activities. Flexible schedules are always listed in recruiting advertisements and promised during the interview. However, a typical scenario has that same employee being berated when they request time off for their upcoming school event. Their manager or scheduler doesn't seem to be aware of this flexible schedule promise. Often times it's the same person who did the interview who has the case of amnesia. This scene when routinely played out ends up with the employee quitting.

Flexible scheduling will give you access to quality teens. Teenagers who are multi-tasking between work, hobbies, academics and family events are well rounded and able to deliver the performance you want.

So why does it so often not play out? Here are a few reasons:

• Not enough employees and you are forced to schedule everyone.

• No communication with employees about current conditions and priority to schedule everyone.

• Flexible scheduling is over promised by interviewer and in recruiting advertising.

• No criteria for when an employee must submit requests for time off or what can be asked for.

• No unified commitment between all owners, managers and supervisors.

What can you do?

- Employ more teens than you are used to, having each work less hours per week. Then you can focus on employing teens that are involved with other activities.

- Establish time frames for when requests for time off must be submitted.

- Put the responsibility of filling shifts on the employee who has the request.

- Have different criteria for teens that have received a promotion and have more responsibility. Flexible schedules may not be available for certain positions and roles. That can be a condition of a new position or increased responsibility.

- Do not over promise flexible schedules simply to be able to improve recruiting.

- All managers must enforce equally.

You're in charge. Flexible scheduling does not mean employees get to come and go as they please. If you align your jobs with the expectations of teens, you will experience attitudes of loyalty and appreciation.

SET GOALS AND EMPOWER

Empowering teens with more responsibility and goal setting may seem counter-intuitive for many. I often hear employers commenting on how irresponsible teens are and how they can't handle even the basic responsibility and workplace tasks they've been given.

Today's teens are the most knowledgeable ever. Not only have they been exposed to more information than ever before, but they also have been hard-wired to know how to instantly access relevant facts, data and ideas.

Turn them loose and make them part of the solution. When teens are micro-managed and not able to function in a way that is natural for them, they'll disconnect from your expectations.

If you have a challenge you can't solve, get your teenage staff involved in the process. Give them the background they need, limits to function within, and a vision of what a successful outcome looks like. Let them come back to you with their solutions. You have nothing to lose and will be amazed at the outside of the box approaches you will receive.

Provide Incentives for Performance

Teens show up with a "what's in it for me" attitude. Performing routine tasks consistently, without a cause and effect to their performance, generates apathy. You want them to perform at an optimal level when business levels are at their highest. In their mind they have no reason to step up their game during these periods.

Provide an incentive for a teen employee to participate in achieving the goals you have established. I know that some of you are thinking that they should already be working hard for you. That's what you pay them for. This is one of those paradigm shifts that needs to occur to fully motivate a teen to participate in your business success. Build it into your budget, program and business model.

Be creative. This needs to be "win-win" and honestly the business will always "win" more than the hourly team member. Incentives do not have to cost much, and can even be free of expense. They can be earned individually or by a work group who has attained a team goal.

Every business has benchmark measurements. Increasing and/or attaining targeted levels of sales volume, item unit sales, productivities and special offers are easy to understand. But everything can be measured, and the adage of "what gets measured will improve" applies.

What do you want to improve? You can reward employees for attendance, uniform and grooming compliance, recruiting, line speed, customer counts, product quality standards, customer comment card ratings, just to name a few.

Get them involved in the process, communicate status and results, and provide a tangible incentive. Later in this chapter is a list of prizes that resonate with teens. Don't forget other assets you have that may be free to you, but high value for them. Consider a preferred parking space for a period of time, increased discounts (or free) on what you sell, lunch with local celebrity you have access to, paid day off, trip to a local amusement park or sporting event, or any other idea you can conjure up.

Following are two separate success stories we experienced:

Beach Bottles: For years we offered a plastic, reusable, souvenir beverage container. Our sales levels never reached anywhere close to what other similar attractions had. We made excuses about the weather and how our customers didn't want take home items. We instituted an incentive program to get our crew to sell more of this specific menu item. We included their feedback in the design of program. The result speaks for itself. We had been averaging approximately 10,000 units a year. In the first year of new program we sold over 50,000 and now average 75,000 annually. We won! They won! Good suggestive selling habits were acquired that transferred over to other items without an incentive.

Crew Search: We used to spend thousands of dollars annually to advertise positions we had available. That was typically spent in classified ads and print advertising in local newspapers. In addition to this, we would attend job fairs and promote at schools. It was an expensive, intensive and unfortunately, an ineffective approach. We still didn't have enough crew, and our expenses continued to increase. We instituted an internal recruitment program paying our current employees to be recruiters. Crew Search has been a phenomenal success. Each employee can earn up to $100 for every employee they recruit and we hire. There is criteria established about the length of time the new employee has to work and performance levels for both employees, before the recruiting bonus is paid. Today we spend absolutely nothing in local papers. Our employees have an additional income opportunity, they recruit their friends, and the workplace environment has improved. Everybody wins!

RECOGNIZE POSITIVE BEHAVIORS

Have you ever lamented about all of the ways that today's teens don't match up to you or others when you were that age? Are you always on the lookout for the next screw up so you can pounce on your teenage employee to let them know about their most recent mistake?

If you want to improve employee performance, forget about the constant vigilance about what they are doing wrong. **Catch them doing something right!** Even at the expense of telling them one more thing they did wrong. Every time they perform at the level you want to see repeated, let them know! Be specific about what they did to your satisfaction. They will respond to this type of interaction in a positive way. Build a foundation on compliments and they will be motivated to improve in other areas at work.

INSTANT PRIZE PROGRAMS

Taking recognition of positive behaviors to the next level is supporting that effort with instant rewards. If you have prizes and incentives that your employees can earn, the redemption period needs to be short term. A teen doesn't past Friday night, so a week is acceptable, a month is far too long, and daily or on the spot is best. The quicker a reward can be earned the higher the level of participation and impact.

Star Cards: Our business has a high degree of seasonality. For decades we celebrated the end of summer and promoted an "end of season" party for our employees. We touted it for months, acquired prizes that were on display, and had incentives attached to it to grow retention. It was a tradition that we believed made us better employers.

Our results were changing. School calendars weren't the same, extra curricular activities were higher priorities, and employees weren't motivated to work longer to win prizes, and those that did seemed less appreciative. Based on our new beliefs and understanding of teens, we cancelled this event. This was a big decision for us. The money we spent for this event was re-budgeted. We created what we call the Star Card, which is a scratch off card that gives employees instant winners and chances at larger prizes. How do they receive a Star Card? They are issued when we "catch them doing something right." Our supervisors write on the card the specific positive action that occurred.

It has been an overwhelming success in creating an improved work environment, employee motivation and productivity.

The 7 C's for Teenage Prizes and Incentives

1. Cars (Gas/Washes)
2. Clothes
3. Concerts
4. CD's
5. Certificates/Cards
6. Cinema
7. Cash

One additional 'C' – Customized. The above incentives, and others that you use, can all be enhanced by customizing them. Teens have been raised in a "have it your way" world. Their drinks are made uniquely for them at Starbucks. Their Facebook pages are created to reflect their character and lifestyle. Computers, the internet and cell phones have made available an endless amount of customized content.

I recently read of a quick service chain that was using customized shoes as an incentive. Nike, Converse and Vans allow consumers to create one-of-a-kind shoes by selecting materials, color and design. This is a genius idea, and also very successful in motivating employees.

PROMOTE QUICKLY

Teens want their contributions to count and they will get cynical quickly if they see what they believe to be inequity occurring. If through their eyes, what they see is that they are capable and their abilities aren't being used, it's just a short amount of time until they are working somewhere else.

We had an archaic policy regarding promoted positions. We placed a higher priority on tenure than on performance. We didn't take advantage of what many teens could deliver. Our policy did nothing but encourage turnover. Today we look first to performance, interest and commitment, and will promote quickly to ensure we keep our best teens.

If you don't have promoted positions, identify skilled tasks that you can assign responsibility to your best people. They'll stay with you longer.

PROVIDE VARIETY

Patience is not a virtue with today's teens. To say they bore easily is an understatement. Be cognizant of the functions and tasks individuals regularly do. If there is never any variety, do what you can do to create some change of pace at work. A little cross training goes a long way to build bench strength and makes you more flexible.

NOT JUST THEIR ATTITUDE...
WHAT ABOUT YOURS?

I've primarily focused on feeding the attitudes of your teenage employees. With that said, I can't think of anything that can have a bigger effect on a teen's attitude than your attitude! A condescending, disrespectful attitude showing no personal interest towards your teen employees will send them out the door, and working down the street.

I'll be the first to admit that it can be hard to maintain a positive, outgoing, caring and personal attitude. But if you have a young workforce it's a discipline you are going to need to excel at if you want teenage employees to serve your interest at work.

Getting a teen's attitude in line with your needs may be a moving target. But you are always in control of yours, and it's the one small thing you, and your managers, can do on a daily basis that can have a huge impact.

Following is a quote from Charles Swindoll about attitude:

The longer I live, the more I realize the impact of attitude on life. Attitude, to me, is more important than facts. It is more important than the past, the education, the money, than circumstances, than failure, than successes, than what other people think or say or do. It is more important than appearance, giftedness or skill. It will make or break a company... a church... a home. The remarkable thing is we have a choice everyday regarding the attitude we will embrace for that day. We cannot change our past... we cannot change the fact that people will act in a certain way. We cannot change the inevitable. The only thing we can do is play on the one string we have, and that is our attitude. I am convinced that life is 10% what happens to me and 90% of how I react to it. And so it is with you... we are in charge of our Attitudes."

I can't think of anything else that will have a larger positive impact on a teen than the attitude that is directed towards them by an adult.

Recognition = Retention

Demonstrating a positive attitude yourself, and aligning your programs to feed the attitudes of a teenager will benefit their performance and your bottom line. Much of focusing on their attitudes is providing them with continuous recognition and attention.

Improved retention is one of the benefits of your new teen focused management style and with the cost of turnover skyrocketing you'll see the financial results of this new approach. As mentioned earlier in this book, it has been determined that the cost of turnover for an entry-level employee exceeds $3,000.

Often times employers don't calculate the indirect costs of employee turnover. It's easier to access the direct costs of recruiting, interviewing, training and uniforms. But the reduction in productivity and customer service can become the lion's share of the expense to replace an entry-level employee.

In our business, we have often experienced big swings in sales, when all other criteria would have suggested only a nominal difference should have occurred. The reason is always because a trained employee was working one day followed by an inexperienced person the next. For us it is hundreds of dollars in sales a day. Improving our retention and capturing those sales justifies our expense and commitment to managing teens for peak performance.

Workforce Management magazine reported that McDonald's restaurants, with reduced turnover of 30%, increased sales by $200,000 annually.

If recognition equals retention, then I'd say it's time to look at how you dish out rewards, praise and responsibility to your teenage employees.

CHAPTER 7

Verbal, Video & Visual Communication – *Utilize It*

On average, teens spend over 7 hours a day in front of a TV or video screen

This may sound like a no brainer, but we all know that teenagers spend a lot of time in front of a video screen. This includes watching their favorite MTV show or playing a video game on TV, exploring YouTube, surfing the internet on their computer and at the same time chatting with friends and hanging out in their Facebook site, or on their iPhones where they can listen to music, watch videos and play with their latest App.

Recent studies have indicated that over 7 hours a day, and rising, is spent in front of a video screen by this age group. Over 20,000 hours of television has been watched by the time a teen has turned 18 years old. The use of video and digital visual images is how the majority of information is taken in by a teen.

Most of these technologies weren't created or accessible to the masses just a mere five years ago. That means that for every teenager you currently employ, all of these technologies have been a normal part of their teenage existence.

It has touched every element of their lives on a *daily* basis. It's as normal and practical for them as it was for us to switch from the rotary dial to touch tone phones, yet its impacts don't compare. These new technologies have *become* the lives of a younger generation. Communication, information, entertainment, socializing, relationships and shopping have all experienced a major transformational shift through these recent innovations.

Employers need to determine the practical ways that are going to evolve and enhance programs and the workplace, in a manner that gets a positive response from young employees. To improve communication and retention of information, adjustments need to be made in methods of delivery. The payoff is a more motivated workforce prepared to serve your customers!

In his book *Megatrends*, John Naisbitt predicted nearly thirty years ago that the more "high tech" we become, there will be an increasing need for "high touch." I believe that today's teens have an innate desire for personal interaction. They need to connect with people not just through a website or cell phone text. They need to be in the presence of other people, to hear their names, to be mentored and to be encouraged.

In the workplace this comes from verbal interaction with teen employees. The words of a manager are powerful. They can lift a person up and build loyalty, or knock them down and build distrust. Teenagers are more sensitive to this type of interaction than ever before. Simply knowing and using their names communicates that they matter and you care.

The following will have you succeeding in communicating with *today's* teens utilizing verbal, video and visual strategies;

USE NAMES & NICKNAMES

Everyone likes to hear his or her names, and that's especially true today of a young employee. It's the most basic recognition that we can receive or give. Perhaps, the more significant point is the impact of NOT remembering someone's name or getting it wrong.

This is such a simple, basic, and personal interaction skill. You need to mandate that anyone who has influence in your organization meets everyone and uses first names. Do not get focused on titles, responsibilities or tenure. This is about valuing people for being people. Eye contact, a smile and a focused question will build commitment to your company. Today's teens require being recognized and remembered, often times over and over again.

> **Whatever their friends call them is the name you need to use**

Be sure to use their nickname. Do not have nametags printed that say "Robert" if their friends call them "Bobby." Capture this on the employment application or definitely during the interview. They will always be disconnected and view themselves as an outsider if you aren't using their correct name. Whatever their friends call them is the name you need to use.

Affirm the Positive

This is an age group that has consistently been rewarded just for participating, without emphasis being placed on results or personal responsibility. Growing up, their sports teams may have never "lost" in fear of damaging their self-esteem.

You can either attempt to undo some sixteen years of their environment and train them your way, or you can swim with the flow. I say go with the path of efficiency and least resistance. Many teens simply do not know how to respond to criticism. Parents, coaches and teachers have removed this method of development from their repertoire. Employers on the other hand have not, and that creates conflict and frustration.

Overemphasize affirming the positive in their behavior and performance. Praise in public and correct the problem in private. In business you cannot ignore areas that require improvement. Problems must be corrected. Often times it's not what you say, but how you say it.

Smaller and Less Complicated

Less is more when it comes to communicating. Streamline anything you have in print so that the salient points don't get lost. This does not mean to compromise on your values or any tenets that you hold as important. In fact this is an opportunity to clarify these issues so that you focus on the most important items for your business success.

Applications: Don't make your employment application long drawn out affairs. Capture the information you want that determines whether they qualify for an interview. Everything else can be captured when they come in for the interview. If a teen leaves with an employment application that is a project to complete, they may very well set it aside. If recruiting is a challenge, you will have lost the ability to speak with a qualified candidate.

Handbooks: You need to have employee handbooks. Conditions of employment and policies must live in one central place. Obtaining signatures that indicate understanding of the included information is a legal necessity. However, if you are expecting retention on the content, again less is more, if it's being delivered in print. There may be a way to say the same thing with a lot less words. You may have outdated policies and guidelines that can be eliminated or revised. Graphics, charts and photos can replace the written word and create white space.

Memos: Any type of current communication to the entire workforce needs to be short and to the point without room for confusion. Use of color, white space and graphics will enhance readership and retention. The area where memos are posted should be approachable and organized but obvious that it changes with new information on display to read.

TEXT, EMAIL & VIDEO FOR COMMUNICATION

When opportunities exist to remove information that is on paper, it should be seriously considered. Collect email addresses and at the minimum reinforce important messages through email. Texting has already far surpassed email as the primary communications tool for teens. Get permission to send out last minute updates by text. You'll have confidence it was at least read.

Communicating company information to employees over video is also more effective than having it read on paper. Consider where you could place a video monitor with employee content to be viewed.

We installed a flat screen monitor in our lobby where all employees clock in for work. Like most businesses we had our bulletin board where we placed current and relevant information. Of course we knew that it was seldom read and rarely absorbed. Now, through the monitor, we run an approximately three minute repeating slide show. The content is photos of employees having fun at work (that we change regularly) and scanned in memos/announcements of the same information that we were putting on the bulletin board. Music is playing throughout the slide show. What we experienced is that all employees are attracted to it and watch it. The music, photos and video screen are a natural lure. And, the workplace information that we communicate is read and retained.

Another use for video is communicating your recruiting message. It is inexpensive to create a short video that highlights all the positives of working with your company. Video gets you consistent delivery of this information. Once the video is produced you can email it to prospective applicants, post it to be viewed on your website, or used as a television commercial. All of these methods are cost effective and support internal recruitment programs.

I never thought we'd ever run a commercial on television about jobs we had available for high school students. We became aware of an opportunity to sponsor a show on a small local cable channel. It was the high school "Game Of The Week" broadcast, and we used the theme of the "League Leader In Student Employment." It was a somewhat hokey add but to a very targeted audience. Students, as well as parents, were loyal viewers. It has been a very successful strategy for us to be top of mind as a student employer. We received by far more feedback on this "video" message than any of our prior recruiting methods.

FACEBOOK FAN PAGE:

Creating a Facebook page that your employees can connect to is becoming the most optimum way to deliver information and to obtain feedback. It is amazing how many, and how quickly employees respond to any post we place. This isn't the sole place to put all mandatory communications, but it is a place that will support and enhance that. The success of this for communicating information this way is just going with the flow. It is the most convenient and relevant way of communicating that your staff know.

VIBRANT WORKPLACE

Teens get bored easily and require constant stimulation. Anything that you can do to keep your workplace fresh, colorful and personalized will create a positive attitude. Colors can be a strong influencer and paint is cheap. Insure that your "back of the house" is as fresh, clean and colorful as what you have for customers.

The simplest approach to achieve this is to have a digital photo board/wall. Don't give up control, but let it be employee managed. Everyone has a digital camera. Photos of coworkers having fun at work, and these same people enjoying times away from work, will create an identity between your employee and their job. It should be updated and expanded regularly.

WORKPLACE FLAIR

Young people want to individualize themselves as much as possible. Flair is an identifier that employees can wear as part of their work attire. It is a public way to highlight certain areas of responsibility, skills, abilities and recognition earned. It can be a part of a nametag, a pin or sewn onto the uniform. Flair can create goals for other employees to strive towards achieving.

APPLICATIONS POSTED ONLINE

Employment applications should be posted online. Even if it seems like a foreign concept, this is easy to have implemented.

Easier access to an application will have you reaching prospective applicants that you won't see otherwise. As high school and college students are searching for and considering employment options, their ability to "close the deal" and submit an application will increase your recruiting numbers. If they have to call for more information, have an application mailed, or need to stop by to pick one up, in all likelihood they'll move on to an employer who has established themselves in this manner.

It also gives applicants that live out of town the ability to apply for work. We employ a lot of college students who line up their summer jobs before coming home from school. If we did not have an online presence with applications, we'd miss out. We receive over 80% of our applications online.

WORK SCHEDULES POSTED ONLINE

Posting a work schedule online is a service to employees, improves attendance and connects you with parents. Privacy concerns are dealt with by requiring a password or employee number for access. Online schedules reinforce the hard copy that you continue to display.

I was a hold-out on implementing our online schedule. I suppose I was showing my age but I just didn't see the necessity. But we did begin posting our schedules online and it was an instant success. After an initial communication to our crew members, they naturally went there. We could tell by how many visitors were going to that web page how broad the acceptance was. Perhaps the biggest surprise for all of us was the value that parents saw. On those rare occasions when our schedules were unavailable online our phone would begin to ring. Not from crew members but from their parents. This gave us an ally at home.

Scheduling software today provides for a lot of employee interaction. There are shift trade boards, direct links to scheduling manager, time off request capabilities. Our scheduling time has been cut in half, and our shifts are always filled. Once an employee had the ability to be responsible for filling any shift they couldn't work, they instantly owned that responsibility. They could do it from their own computer or their iPhone. Another insight that came from online scheduling was that we could see when an employee went online to check their schedule. We learned that more times than not, schedules were checked in very "non traditional" times, like between midnight and 4:00am. Incidentally, when our schedules are complete, we automatically text out schedules to each employee.

Employee Website
It's probably a foregone conclusion by now that you need an online presence. A website for your employees should be as important as a website for customers. There is a natural tendency for teens to go the web for information. If you want to communicate effectively, you need to be there.

In addition to posting employment applications and work schedules, you can replicate employee handbooks, policies, procedures and other training materials for easy access and review. An employee website bulletin board will give co-workers a place to check in with each other as well as being another way for you to communicate with them. You can have tests online that measure an employees understanding of policies and procedures, and run contests that encourage site visitation and use.

Computer & DVD Training
Moving training materials and methods to computer based, and using DVD and video will improve your overall message, retention and results. It may not replace, but will definitely enhance the one-on-one time currently spent.

There are many computer based training modules that have built in testing and tracking. Most of these have the ability to be customized. Based on the industry you are in, check with your trade association about members who provide computer-based training.

DVD training is an improvement over an individual presenting the same information, over and over again. It gives you consistency in your training message to all employees, and your trainer is able to spend more time on fine tuning results and conducting follow up.

Build an inventory of customized video of specific tasks that are important to your business. Start with the most challenging or confusing work functions you have. It's a real skill to break down a function and communicate to someone else. Creating video will force you to do that.

There's a company in eastern Tennessee, *Pal's Sudden Service*, that is the only restaurant business to ever be recognized with the Malcolm Baldrige National Quality Award. Pal's does a lot of things very well. One of their training innovations is breaking down the tasks of every function in one of their restaurants to sixty to ninety second video segments. They load this video content onto an iPod and their employees can have it with them while they are performing the task. Watch it, do it and watch it again. It has been a very successful training strategy. Teen employees respond well to the use of this familiar technology and are more inclined to use it and learn.

We have now adopted this short video clip training technique.

Another strength of this program is moving the training out of the "classroom" and into the workplace. Everything becomes much more real and understandable. Recent models of some Point of Sale Systems have the ability to play video. Having this type of training content at the fingertips of your employees is invaluable.

* * * * *

Improving the way you communicate with teens begins with understanding and accepting the ways in which they naturally communicate. It has totally changed in just the last few years.

Utilizing verbal, video and visual communications techniques that teenagers are used to and comfortable with will improve your business, and your relationship with them. Like other ways to connect with teenagers, this may require you to get educated on these techniques and technologies. Undoubtedly it will look quite a bit different from when you were a teen, but will provide a more efficient pathway to reach today's teens.

CHAPTER 8

Education... Not Just Training – *Emphasize It*

Training Is the How. Education Is the Why.

It's a fact that the majority of teens today do not get the workplace preparedness training they used to. I understand that exceptions do exist, however the majority of teenagers do not show up with an understanding of what's expected at work. It's not their fault and they could never understand the comparison. It reflects the environment they have been raised in and the lack of workplace information and advice they've been given.

When I was a teen, work habits and job skills information came from parents, teachers, counselors and coaches. All adults seemed to support the notion that any job was a good job. Show up and do what you're told. The boss was always right. A part time job was a right of passage and a part of growing up. Whether it was to raise some spending money or check out potential careers, everyone had a job.

Even though the labor market and economy of the last two years have made having a job a higher priority, in today's world parents are more likely to side with their child and not support commitments made, and the expectations of the business owner/manager. They may have a corporate bias due to being laid off, outsourced, downsized, or in some other way impacted by or unexpectedly put out of work.

With reduced budgets, teachers deal with larger class sizes and less support services. School safety concerns and student discipline challenges requires more attention. These issues drive a focus to address only academic basics and educational legal requirements. Finding time to be a proponent of the values of an entry-level job is rare.

School work-experience and career counselors are a shrinking profession, and those that exist have to fit in these responsibilities around a multitude of other duties. Many schools have had no other choice but to eliminate these positions.

Coaches used to literally order their kids to get a job and would never intentionally tell a student athlete to not uphold their responsibilities at work. Part time jobs helped to build teamwork and discipline, both transferable to the sports team. Today coaches exert tremendous pressure and influence as sports have taken a far larger societal role. In our experience today, coaches do not advocate on behalf of the employer.

Add into this mix the reality that students aren't proactively searching for this information on their own. Entry-level jobs are incongruent with the multi-million dollar lifestyles of their celebrity heroes. Through ignorance, they impatiently believe they will go directly from homeroom to the boardroom.

There is an irony in all of this. On one hand there is a real lack of information about work being taught to teens. On the other hand, this is an age group that will exceed expectations when they've acquired fundamental knowledge.

Earlier in this book I addressed our observation that teens can be inspired and self motivated. Our experience was that in those activities that they wanted to excel in, they were extremely knowledgeable on every aspect. You may recall that in Santa Cruz, California it is surfing that inspires our youth. Our employees who excelled in surfing could rattle off facts about the effects of tides, winds, currents and waves, temperatures, type of board required and safety concerns. They were indeed *educated* on surfing.

The point is that they want to know more, can handle large quantities of information, and when they have it they will perform at the highest, most optimum level.

So who is going to educate teens so that they are ready to go to work?

THE NEW BUSINESS REQUIREMENT

With teens showing up less prepared than in the past, what's an employer to do? Ignoring the situation and changing nothing will only lead to continued frustration, as well as teens that are less prepared for work in their future.

I believe that a new requirement of business is to take an active role in the education of employees. Instead of expecting that someone else will teach job skills, it will be up to employers. Build it into your training and orientation programs. Materials and curriculum can be obtained from local high schools through what were their work experience programs. Make this type of information available to all of your employees. It will be the first time many have ever seen anything on basic work ethics.

What are the types of job skills I'm talking about? Following are basic work ethic topics. Teach them, along with why they are important in your workplace, and you will see productivity soar. You will also be providing a community service, as you build up teens for a better future.

First Job 101
- How to complete an application
- Communicating effectively, Interpersonal & People Skills
- Dependability
- Tardiness, Absenteeism, & Attendance
- Initiative
- Responsibility
- Reliability
- Honesty
- Honoring Commitments

First Job 102
Following are additional education topics that you may consider making available, along with potential resources.

Career Building: Focus on your industry and search out your trade associations and publications.

Financial Skills Education: Through your bank, credit card company or non-profit organizations that focus on youth, you will find financial skills literacy materials available.

Health and Wellness Education: Your workers compensation carrier or local hospital foundation will have adequate,materials as well as classes on this subject.

Following are some additional places you can locate content and materials:

Local High School & Colleges: Many have lost the budget and resources to teach these topics, but typically will have materials you can use for free.

Trade Associations: Your business or organization may already be a member of an industry trade association that would have information and support materials available for basic work training. This may be an untapped resource and benefit of your membership. Start with our local Chamber of Commerce.

Junior Achievement: Their focus is geared towards promoting work ethics, job value and the free enterprise system to a younger market. There are additional non-profit associations that have the same mission. Check out: www.ja.org

Have realistic expectations. Just because you are being a responsible employer by proactively making this life-education information available, do not expect that all of your young workforce will rush to utilize it. Many will not, at least not initially. Nevertheless, there will be some that do take advantage of it, and their commitment, loyalty, advocacy and participation in your company will grow.

By the way, include all the above information on your employee website by listing links and uploading documents.

· ·

Make education one of your values and a primary component of your employment brand.

· ·

MUST KNOW THE WHY & PROVIDE REASONS AND PURPOSE

Teens today ask a lot of questions. They just don't take their marching orders and carry them out without question. They ask <u>Why</u>.

Why do I have to do that?
Why do I have to do what she says?
Why do I have to work with them?
Why do I have to work that shift?
Why do I have to take my break then?
Why do I have to wear this uniform?
Why do we sell this product?
Why…Why…Why?

The natural inclination when faced with this inquisition is to respond with a short answer, leaving them with the direction of "just do it." However, when you take a step back and fill their curiosity, amazing things can happen.

Teens don't accept facts at face value. They are used to having supportive data to back up whatever new information has been made available. In their entire lives, they have been able to "google it" and instantly locate information. It's a habit they take for granted. Since they can't google why you prescribe a certain procedure at work, it can raise uncertainty for them. It leaves them asking why, giving you the opportunity to provide them with an answer.

With any first time task, provide them with the background and reason behind it. Make it an educational opportunity. Your training procedures and company policies should be written to include this information. Your employee handbook ought to be full of the "why it's important" answers. It will positively impact the quality of your training, and insure that everyone in your company has the same information. It will force you to be clear on the need for certain policies and procedures. If there are routinely asked questions, put those in the form of a *Frequently Asked Questions* list and make that available in all appropriate areas.

Teens will appreciate having an increased understanding, and you will see results in customer service, product/service quality, employee motivation and contribution.

Set your workforce up for success.

Providing reasons and purpose is not giving in and letting teens win. It is a strategic adjustment on your part to achieve your goals and add to your business success.

HIRING VIDEO
A perfect place to start is a video that you use for recruiting new employees, and to be used prior to any prospective new employee being hired.

In this video you need to "tell it like it is." What is expected of them, what the benefits are, and why it matters. In the video we put together for our company we used current employees as the "actors" to tell the story of hard work, busy days, working weekends, etc. They also shared the benefits of working with our company.

This approach has been the perfect starting point for us in "educating" our young workforce. The video can be viewed at anytime by visiting our website, and the feedback we have received has been very positive in regards to painting a picture what is expected as well as what to expect.

Never Assume Anything

Do not assume that even the most basic of tasks can be accomplished without direction. Teens need to be set up for success. If they haven't performed a task before, make sure they have received skills training and have been educated on the purpose.

A friend of mine tells the story of sending a new employee into the kitchen to clean dirty dishes. After about thirty minutes he went in to check on her. She was standing there staring at the sink in wonderment and disbelief, not able to figure out why the water kept disappearing. She had never washed a dish in her life!

Use that true story as an example. Her lack of knowledge on this particular "life skill" of plugging the drain, I'm afraid represents a myriad of other tasks we used to be able to take for granted. Do not leave anything to chance without the adequate training.

If left to figure out for themselves, teens may fail at even the most basic of work functions. The impact on your business could range from an inconvenience to an expense you could have controlled. More importantly, teens aren't used to "failing." Finding themselves in this situation creates embarrassment in an uncomfortable situation. Through eventually quitting, they'll retreat to their comfort zone of friends and home.

PARTIES WITH A PURPOSE

Connect fun and education. I wrote in an earlier chapter on the value of social events attached to work. Making these a *Party with a Purpose* will present the educational component more palatable, attractive and memorable.

Through tests, contests, scavenger hunts, and Q&A, you can highlight your company's history, values, products, service, management team and current initiatives and future plans, in a fun and enjoyable way.

Think outside the box when it comes to methods of educating your teen staff.

SUGGESTION PROGRAMS

Most companies have some sort of employee suggestion program, or at the minimum are welcome to having their employees share their insights and ideas on serving customers better.

An organized, well promoted, branded, high profile suggestion program will yield a specific benefit towards educating your workforce. Besides generating new ideas to make a business better, it gives you the opportunity to respond to all of your employees through answering these suggestions. Posting the questions and answers on bulletin boards and your website or emailing to your entire team, everyone gets the same answer, purpose and reason, that's associated with the submitted question or idea.

TRACK PERFORMANCE

Focusing on catching people doing something right, even at the expense of what they may have done wrong is still the most efficient and effective approach to motivate a young workforce.

> Have regularly scheduled
> workplace performance reviews

However, you should have a process in place where you do track employee performance. Capture as much specific detail as you can about their performance. Attendance, grooming standard compliance, acceptance to policies and procedures and how they respond to supervision and co-workers are a few examples of what to track. You are apt to not collect 100% of what's occurred. But you will get enough to tell a story.

Examples of workplace performance to track;

Attendance
Tardiness
Grooming Standards

Policy and procedure compliance
Supervisor cooperation
Internal & External Customer comments
Cash management

When you sit down with your employee and are able to go over very specific workplace experiences, a framework is created for the education that needs to occur.

Don't use these facts to let them know what they have done wrong, use these to educate on;

Why these issues are important
What the impacts are
Who it effects
How to improve their performance

COMMUNICATIONS:

For sure a well communicated workforce will perform at higher levels than those left in the dark to guess and figure things out for themselves. With today's teens and young adults, "how" you communicate may be more important as "what" you communicate.

Information should be distributed in multiple ways, and you should consider all or most of the following;

- Post information and distribute materials
- Create a newsletter
- Email information
- Text your employees
- Set up an employee Facebook site
- Post on your employee website

Improved communications increases motivation

EMPLOYEE WEBSITE

This is THE place to have all workplace information and becomes your educational hub.

Following are some of the purposes for considering using an employee website;

Download training materials: Any materials you create, from your employee manual to updated policies and procedures, should be available on website and able to be viewed or downloaded.

Include links: Allow your employees to easily link to other websites of businesses that support, you or that you want to support. Links to organizations that provide educational information should be included.

Check their work schedules: Post your schedules online and make your employee website the portal for access. This will drive traffic from your entire staff.

Training videos: Training videos can be streamed on the website for viewing.

Information on health, wellness and finances: The types of information that was addressed in the "First Job 102" section of this workbook should be on website. It may be as simple as links to the providers of this info.

Employees suggestion program: Employees should be able to easily make suggestions or to submit workplace questions.

Track Performance: Whether it's points for an awards program or points they have incurred for workplace performance, these can be made confidentially available on site.

Employee Polling: If you want ongoing feedback regarding how you are doing in the eyes of your employees, utilize polling software and regularly query your employees with timely questions.

Email the Boss: By a click of a button, employees should be able to drop "the boss" a note, question or comment.

Management Bio's: The background, along with a photo, of your leadership team should be included.

Employee Photos, Quotes and Testimonials: Let your employees be seen and heard.

> Access to info on your employee
> website is available 24/7.
> Whenever they want to take it in.

Employee websites work for several key reasons, that include the fact that they can access information 24 hours a day/7 days a week, when they want to, and not just while they are at work. This feeds their desire for individuality.

This is an age group who lives online and delivering information in this manner is simply a necessary adjustment that will serve your interests. Consider it the piece that brings your entire education initiative to life.

View your employee website as a "storefront." To maintain interest and traffic, regularly change the appearance, content, and reasons for visiting. Providing password protection for privacy and confidentiality can be incorporated.

TRAINING IS THE HOW. EDUCATION IS THE WHY.

Training is essential. Businesses need checklists, processes and procedures. Everything needs to be written down. Training insures consistency among employees and locations and assures that your customers are receiving what you've promised. Employee compliance to your training standards is essential and should never be compromised.

You want people working for you that understand your procedures, and can also think for themselves, as well respond appropriately to the unexpectedness of business. Educating them on the why is critical. If you prepare teens to know the purpose of your rules, and reasoning behind them, they will then deliver service at a level you have never seen.

I once heard that the person who only knows the how, will always work for the person who knows the why.

Do yourself and teenage employees a favor and make it a priority to *educate* them at work.

CHAPTER 9

Style Matters – *Realize It!*

Teens don't quit companies.
They quit people.

Style is how employees *look*, the *image* of your company and how they are *treated* at work. These three issues hit on the core of attracting and motivating today's teens. If you miss on these issues, the best you can hope to be is a short-term stop on a teenager's job journey. It will be an expensive cycle of frustration.

How you present yourself as a company is equally important. Your recruiting ads, training materials, business appearance, community involvement and management behavior all creates an image in the minds of a teenager.

Following are areas to consider as you review how your employees look, how you present yourself, and how they are treated.

HOW TEENS LOOK AT WORK...
GROOMING & UNIFORMS
Teens care about how they look. Individualism is currently at an all time high with teens. Uniforms shouldn't embarrass

your staff, and grooming policies should be routinely reviewed for relevance. Conversely, work attire does not need to be suitable for a fashion show or become a distraction.

This is not a message to change the look of your teenage employees to simply satisfy their ego and peer pressures. There can be a fine line between a company's uniform and grooming standards and the brand message you want communicated to your customers.

I have been to plenty of businesses where it seems no attention has been given to how an employee looks. Visible tattoos, multiple piercings, spiked multi-colored hair along with whatever clothes they could find to put on is how the business was represented. In some cases the customer service has been phenomenal and other times far less stellar. I've also been a customer in businesses where employees are uniformed head to toe, with well defined policies against grooming extremes. Even in this scenario, customer service levels can vary.

A question to ponder: What impact will your uniform and grooming standards have if your customers receive poor customer service?

Our business operates within an amusement park. This industry is typically very conservative when it comes to uniforms and grooming, and slow to make adjustments. This is for good reason. Most amusement and theme parks serve a family audience, ranging in age from infant through grandparents. These guests represent the values of communities from distances away. Presenting oneself in a manner that will be acceptable to anyone and everyone is important. Additionally, as large teenage employers, the more latitude you provide on grooming policies can create a management nightmare.

Our policies regularly come up as a point of discussion for review. The vast majority of our customers come from out of town. The Santa Cruz community, where our employees live, is very open-minded and accepting of all fashion trends. You can almost get a tattoo and piercing at a drive-thru!

Through thoroughly communicating the <u>why</u> behind our uniform policy we've been successful with a conservative uniform and grooming policy. We have made some specific refinements to allowable jewelry, hairstyles and nametags that were more popular with our crew. We will continue to review and access impacts of trends, but not respond to fads in teenage styles.

In an effort to provide a makeover for their crew, McDonald's enlisted the assistance of designer Sean "P Diddy" Combs. Their goal was to up the "cool factor" in how their crew looked and felt about their employer. Following are a couple of quotes:

"It's about taking the contemporary look and feel of our restaurants and embodied in our advertising and incorporating that into our employees' business attire," according to McDonald's spokesman Bill Whitman. "The desire is to create uniforms that our crews would want to wear outside the restaurant environment."

It's an effort to update the fast-food giant's image and connect with young employees and customers. It's unclear if the new look will sell more burgers, but experts say cool clothes could help its mass-market image and make its en-

try-level jobs a little more attractive. If the fashion is good, employees will probably see getting the clothes as a good reason to take the job, said Rick Levine, publisher of Made To Measure, a uniform industry trade publication. Lavine continued; "My first job as a freshman in high school was at Long John Silver's, back when they had those little pirate hats and a fake earring," Levine said. "Try to get a kid today to wear that. No way. Now they've all got golf shirts."

Through utilizing a uniform company, purchasing from local clothing stores, or requiring your staff to acquire themselves and wear to your specifications, there are easy ways to update your uniforms.

Consider utilizing a uniform design that comes in different colors or designs, but still represents your company, brand image or message. Let your employees choose which one they want to wear.

At Lagoon Amusement Park in Salt Lake City, they came up with a phenomenal idea that allowed their young employee base to tap into their individuality. Throughout the park, in their retail stores, they sold many different styles, colors and designs of hats. The parks wardrobe department was not providing anything close to the cool factor that the hats available to guests had. It was an instant success. Their hundreds of teenage employees were now able to feel good about what they were wearing and show their personality at the same time. This was a simple idea that had big results.

You need to decide how you want the pendulum to swing. Just be prepared to proactively communicate why you have selected the uniforms and grooming standards that you have, and why that matters to your customers, and your overall business positioning and success.

Lastly, every business has to determine what uniform policy and grooming standards will serve the interests of its business, customers and employees. It's a big decision as employee appearance is often a major brand/company identifier. Whatever you decide to do with your grooming standards and uniforms, your teen employee's commitment is essential for success. After that decision has been made, be fair & consistently enforce. Nothing else will doom your program like inconsistent compliance of standards.

HOW TEENS ARE TREATED AT WORK...
SET AN ATTRACTIVE EXAMPLE

Style isn't just uniforms and looks. It's how you carry yourself as a company and how you are represented by supervisors/managers.

As a supervisor of teens, you have tremendous influence on their performance, motivation, retention and lives. How you manage your relationships with these teens is central to success or failure in these areas.

First, as a company you must insure that every manager or supervisor is on board with the commitment of getting the most from today's teens. If you want to initiate new strategies, but even one manager is unwilling to embrace a new approach, your entire effort will be sabotaged. Teens can recognize true authenticity. If one thing is being communicated, but their supervisor's actions delivers an inconsistent message, then you will have wasted your time. The opposite of course is true. If you have 100% buy-in from your leadership team, all you can do is succeed.

Be available. Don't judge. Ask questions. Solicit feedback. Show concern. Be Fair. Recognize effort. Celebrate success. Deliver on what you promise. Don't over-promise. Follow up. These are just some *actions* that can be routinely taken by supervisors that will leave your teens feeling appreciated and treated well.

HOW YOUR BUSINESS IMAGE LOOKS TO TEENS...

BUSINESS IMAGE

Teens want to be a part of organizations that are successful, popular with peers, and provide value. Anything that an employee sees, hears or touches at work defines the image of the business.

Besides your advertising geared for customers, even employment ads and training materials make an impression about your company. Use designs and humor that resonates with teens. The types of quality standards and workplace policies that are in place, and how passionately they are promoted and adhered to, can have a tremendous imaging impact.

Community non-profit groups that you support tell a teen much about your company. To leverage this involvement for an employment benefit, contribute to organizations that a teen can connect with. Better yet, get their feedback and input ahead of time and give them the opportunity to volunteer for the cause.

It matters what a teen thinks about your company. A positive connection will make them extremely loyal, committed and long time employees.

KNOW WHAT'S POPULAR WITH TEENS

The image that a company portrays can be a negative one if you are simply out of sync with what is popular with today's teens. The best of intentions will be wasted if you are behind the times.

Pay attention to how retailers are reaching teens, what they are offering and what is popular. You don't need to like, agree, or even use what you learn, but you'll be better off with the knowledge.

It matters what the popular music, clothes, brands, TV shows are and who are today's top celebrities. Employee incentives and company events can be themed around popular products and programs. The more in tune you are the better your image is with your teen staff.

The most obvious and practical use of staying current with teen fads and trends is for employee incentive programs. I've already addressed the benefits of providing incentives for employee performance. It's effective for motivating this age group. The "right" brands and products are very influential to teens, however, the wrong type of products will generate a poor image of your company, and fall flat on its face. The wrong products for incentives will generate the unintended consequence of not achieving its purpose and making you look bad in the process.

For example, just because you can get a great deal on Sony Walkman CD players does not mean your teenage workforce will care. This is the iPod generation, where nearly 90 percent of all teens own one.

As another example, as I write this, iTunes, the music download site that Apple Computer launched just five years ago, passed Wal-Mart to become the world's largest seller of music. Teenagers have driven this transformation from music store CD's to digital downloads. Things change, and this demonstrates that they change quickly and in a big way. Pay attention and take advantage to motivate your teen workforce.

· ·
Teens don't quit companies.
They quit people
· ·

It's true. Whether it is how teens look, how they are treated, or your businesses image, it's all about the decisions that you make that impact the workplace environment and how teens feel about it.

Mentioned earlier in this book is the true and total cost of turnover. It's expensive, over $3,000 per employee. You can't afford to make poor decisions or have leadership that does not carry out the company's mission.

You have the ability to become the employer of choice. A place that understands what motivates today's teens and then implements those key points into programs, policies and procedures at work. If not, you will be a place for them to hang out long enough until they find an employer they believe to be "cool." It may end up being a case of "perception is reality," but if it doesn't work out, so what. They'll simply move on to another job, and you lose.

CHAPTER 10

WAVES for Teenage Workforce Success

Way of Life – *Create It!*
Attitude – *Feed It!*
Verbal, Visual & Video Communication – *Utilize It!*
Education. . . Not Just Training – *Emphasize It!*
Style Matters – *Realize It!*

The five themes of the WAVES acronym can serve as an overview of how to build and improve programs designed to engage a teenage workforce. It is meant to be versatile enough to meet your current needs and not merely a standardized checklist that may not be pertinent or relevant to your specific issues.

Every business has unique circumstances with regard to employing teens. And today's problem may move to a different challenge tomorrow.

The number one issue we hear about is getting teenage employees to be motivated at work. Wanting them to care, show concern and be interested in the goals of the business. In many areas of the country, recruiting teens has proven to be tremendously difficult and often times retention and managing employee turnover is where emphasis needs to be placed.

Teen employment challenges can also be a moving target. They can change as local economies, demographics and marketplace conditions evolve. Over many years, in our business, we have faced all of the employment priorities.

Whatever your challenge points are, the WAVES system is flexible enough to meet your needs and will work. I've provided you with many solutions able to be enhanced with your personal creativity and knowledge of your employees.

WAVES equals action. Sometimes you just know you have to move forward and do something. When you improve how you recruit, educate, motivate and retain today's teens, the rewards can be extraordinary. To achieve these rewards though, requires a willingness to change.

I pursued this project initially out of our own interest. We employ a lot of teens and we wanted to improve our business. I was encouraged to use this opportunity to share and learn from others, so I gathered facts, experiences, expertise, education and results.

I know that the WAVES system works. We put elements of the program in place for our teenage workforce, and have seen significant and measurable improvements in all the following areas:

Recruiting
Retention
Motivation
Customer Service
Sales

Even though improving our own business is how this journey began, it became increasingly evident there was a growing demand that would benefit all employers of teens. No matter where I went, or whom I spoke with, I either observed or heard frustrations. It was becoming increasingly clear that employers did not have the answers or know what to do. They were shooting in the dark. This was primarily due to a lack of understanding of how today's teens have changed and what it takes to get them to respond.

Times are changing quickly. When I have presented to groups of managers/supervisors in their early twenties, they speak of 16 and 17 year olds like a younger generation. They don't understand these "kids" that are just a half dozen years younger.

Typically the managers were on parallel tracks with the employees. They were so close, yet so far away, from effective solutions. Managers would revert to how they were trained and motivated when they were teens. And teens would go about their duties not even aware of the efforts to motivate them that were being attempted by the manager.

This can have devastating consequences. Following are two quick stories of businesses with dire results.

There was a local, independently owned coffee store that had opened near our home. They had done a great job in designing their location, with a nice ambiance and quality product. My wife and I were very regular customers and we always ordered the same drinks. We used to joke about how every time we came in we were treated as if it was our first visit. No one ever remembered our drink order. They had a young workforce, and often times they would jump down from sitting on the counter as I walked in. Many times I felt as though I was inconveniencing them, as my presence broke up conversations either between coworkers or friends. Then I'd go through the motions of placing the exact order as I had done on almost a daily basis.

They were faced with the uncertain future of Starbucks opening up nearby. After Starbucks did open we stayed committed to supporting the local coffee store. The service level never changed and after some point of disbelief in our customer service, I ventured into the Starbucks. I was immediately greeted with a smile and eye contact and engaged in a brief conversation. I ordered my wife's non-fat latte, and they gave me a coupon for a free drink. Of course I went back. Within a week they knew my name and drink order, and have continued to recognize us on every visit.

Starbucks did not earn our business because they are a multi-national corporation. They did because they made a commitment to educate and engage their employees on the importance of customer service. They understood the lifetime value of a customer and placed a high priority on engaging their workforce to achieve this goal. The local coffee store ended up going out of business. There may have been other factors impacting their decision to close, but I can't help to believe that their inability to connect with their teenage staff to achieve the values and goals of their business was central to the reason.

They could have used the knowledge, background and principles of the WAVES system, to get their young workforce to proactively contribute to their business success.

Another story;

I had become acquainted with a man who had recently left a long career in high-tech to go into business for himself. He had a dream of starting a family business, and along with his son as manager, they became franchisees of two units of a national quick service chain. Through shared community interests we crossed paths regularly and conversations always shifted to business issues. From the start, his number one challenge was staffing. Whether it was quantity, quality or getting his teenage employees to honor the commitments they had made, it had become a point of major frustration. He wanted to work on his business, not in it. But staffing challenges were forcing him to be very much working in it. When shifts went unfilled, often times at the last minute, the only thing he knew to do was to jump in and work the shift. He became increasingly frustrated and burnt out and had lost any passion he had for the business. His dream had become a job… and one he didn't enjoy. The day I walked into one of his locations and he was up on the counter cleaning windows, and greeted me with, "You can buy this place for ten cents on the dollar," I knew the end was near. Ultimately the franchisor took the locations back.

I wish that I had the WAVES system in place back then. He could have used this understanding of today's teens to keep his business, and his dream alive. He was a very intelligent man but did not have the tools to motivate a teenage workforce.

I know there are many other business people that could positively impact the lives of teens as well as their own lives. What they need is a fresh perspective and simpler approach when it comes to managing their teenage employees.

The WAVES for *Teenage Workforce* Success program would do that.

Not all teenage employees are challenging. Some have a tremendous work ethic and the majority has much potential. The numbers may vary by business but following is a breakdown:

10% are phenomenal superstars. Celebrate them and make sure they know how much they are appreciated. Clone them if you can. Certainly find out if they have friends who can work. The biggest risk with these employees is you inadvertently burn them out by relying on them too much.

10% are bad hires. Somehow they slipped through the cracks and got hired. You don't have the time and capability to transform them into productive, responsible employees. Make them someone else's challenge and get rid of them as quickly as possible. Nothing can do more damage to the workplace environment than a bad hire with a bad attitude.

They drag everyone else down with them. You need to pull the weeds and plant the seeds with new hires.

80% have great potential and are ready to be engaged. These are the majority of the teens you hire that are anxious to contribute at work. It is up to you to understand them... not the other way around. They are the ones you are targeting by utilizing WAVES.

Like the Beach Boys song says, "Catch a WAVE and you'll be sitting on top of the world."

How do you catch your first WAVE?

To gain the support and participation of your teenage staff, you should consider transitioning from the Golden Rule to the Platinum Rule.

GOLDEN RULE
Treat others the way
You
Want to be treated

Is replaced with the ...

PLATINUM RULE
Treat others the way
They
Want to be treated

CHAPTER 11

Everyone Can Lead – Leadership 1 0 1
The ability to guide. direct. and influence others

"What do I do now?" is a question I am regularly asked at presentations. It comes from people who have gained a new perspective and understanding of what it takes to motivate their teen staff. They are energized and excited about the possibility of improvements.

My answer to their question is quick and always the same. *Change can occur with leadership.* What I've learned in this quick dialogue exchange is that many of these managers and supervisors don't consider themselves leaders. Therefore they do not have the belief in themselves that they can influence change.

They believe it would be simpler, if they could just start all over with a new slate and not have to undo the past. Life and managing a team of teenage employees, isn't that easy. They need to go back to their place of business and create a new culture with their current employees. They may need to change what they've been doing to introduce new initiatives with WAVES.

Following is an introductory lesson on leadership, designed to effect change. It's leadership 101 for the busy person. Leadership is defined as *the ability to guide, direct and influence others*. Teens will willingly be directed or influenced after trust and respect has been earned.

Consistent application of these principles will place you in that position to gain their support and transition your culture.

The first step is to dispel these three common leadership myths:

TOP 3 LEADERSHIP MYTHS

MYTH # 1: I'M NOT A LEADER

Unfortunately this is how many managers wrongly view themselves. Realize that if you are in a position to impact others, you are a leader! Specifically with teens, you are more influential than you think. Be confident, communicate your vision and ask for feedback.

MYTH #2: LEADERS ARE BORN, NOT MADE

Often time's people confuse leaders and leadership with charismatic individuals who are outgoing and able to deliver a motivating speech. Real leadership comes from those who are quiet, consistent, have a vision and a great attention to detail. That's what impacts change and builds respect. Invest in yourself to develop teens.

MYTH #3: LEADING MEANS BOSSING

To most people bossing means yelling, which is an idea that scares a lot of managers. In my experience, those who yell the most know the least, and they are trying to cover up their own insecurities and inability to deal with situations. Additionally, bossing only delivers short-term results. Leading through serving others has a lasting impact. Grow your job knowledge, delegate, then help others get their work done.

EVERYONE CAN LEAD

Following is an acronym of the word LEAD. These four points are easy-to-remember leadership principles that work amazingly well in influencing teens.

LEAD BY EXAMPLE

You are always on stage and actions really do speak louder than words. Anything you expect from your teen employees needs to be modeled by you. Teens respond to authenticity, and your actions will either build relationships or create distrust. If you say one thing and do another, a commitment to change will be difficult to effect.

EXCITE THEM WITH A CHALLENGE

Change can occur by transferring ownership of responsibility. Give an individual or team of teenage employees a goal to attain, or challenge to solve and let them come up with the solution and action plan. Teens know how to access information and are creative thinkers. When your teen employees participate in the process, the change will become permanent.

Affirm Their Potential — Be Specific

If you want to impact change in the workplace, you'll need the support of your teen staff. You'll get that support if you are recognizing and complimenting good performance. "Good job" can come off as shallow and routinely said, having no impact. Be as specific as you can about what they did right, how it contributes to the workplace, and thank them. This approach will have their productivity skyrocketing and they'll be open to additional future change.

Deliver Honest Feedback

Key: Affirm the person, Correct the problem

Mistakes and areas of performance that require improvement must be corrected. Teen employees will respond to real time, honest feedback. Always build the person up, and be specific on the problem. Separate the person from problem. This approach will create loyalty and open minds to change.

The subject of leadership and managing change is an expansive topic. However, the above four simple points can have you beginning the process of change and implementing elements of the WAVES system, so that you will positively impact the quality of a teen's performance and your business.

Inspect what you Expect

Once you have implemented a procedural change, success is only experienced when you have insisted on staying the course. That is when you will begin to see the culture shift that will reveal itself through automatic results. Don't let any member of your team sabotage your efforts. You need to insist on compliance and *inspect what you expect*. Whatever the improvements are that you are initiating, follow up on the details.

- Are you celebrating a teenager's success?
- Is flexible scheduling occurring?
- Are you "catching them doing something right" and quickly rewarding them for it?
- Have you made sure your leadership team has adjusted their attitude, approach and understanding of being a teenager *today*?
- Are you using photos and video to communicate?
- Are you insuring that an employee is always getting the *why* behind a task?
- Have you challenged your teen employees, and solicited their feedback on ways to achieve company goals?

Those are just a few questions to ask yourself as you are on the pathway to implementing elements of WAVES.

CHAPTER 12

Hiring the Best of Today's Teens & Young Adults
Building Your Foundation

In the last couple of years the national unemployment rate has hovered on one side or the other of 10%. As if that wasn't bad enough, high school and college age employees have been experiencing unemployment rates that exceed 20% on the low end, in just about every area of our nation. A combination of fewer positions, and more competition from an older age group that is struggling to find work or to bolster their income, has taken a direct hit on the young workforce.

The impact of this has had young people scrambling to find jobs that they used to take for granted. And if they have a job, needing to work more hours to cover expenses that they may not have been responsible for in the past. For employers, the greatest impact has been on having a significant increase in job applications.

It's true that a weaker economy has provided many employers with access to a larger group of potential future employees. What I have witnessed often though are unchanged hiring practices. The net result is that it is has just gotten easier to hire more of the *same* people you have hired in the past.

Use the circumstance of today's economy to create a stronger foundation that you can build on for years to come.

Hiring the best of today's teens can be a real challenge, but also a tremendous opportunity. The process you use in selecting who will be on your team can insure that you hire only those applicants that serve your company and your customers the best. Or you can go through the motions and hire whoever applies first, creating frustration, conflict and increased turnover.

· ·

Hiring the best teens available matters to your bottom line.

· ·

In an earlier chapter I went into more detail about the cost of turnover and how expensive it can be, particularly when you factor in a reduction in productivity that new employee brings. Taking a fresh look at your hiring procedures can greatly improve your turnover rate, saving you thousands of dollars.

The pathway to your hiring success includes the following;

- Establishing your needs and the qualities required
- Assessing the applications
- Strategies that separate applications
- The interview environment
- Pre-employment testing
- Orientation and Training success

DEFINE THE JOB AND ESTABLISH YOUR NEEDS

Many organizations aren't clear on what the "perfect employee" looks like. This is an important first step in reducing turnover. This doesn't mean that 100% of every person you hire in the future will always fit into this mold. What it does mean though is that you will at least recognize that you have a strong applicant in front of you that needs to be hired. It also will identify the strengths and areas of improvement that an applicant possesses, allowing you to be aware of, and focus on, those areas of improvement.

Top qualities of a teenage employee. Following are some attributes and skills you will want to be on the lookout for;

- Well groomed
- Ability to communicate
- People Skills (eye contact and a smile)
- Basic math, reasoning and comprehension
- Thorough, complete and neat application
- Ambition
- Courtesy
- Trustworthiness
- Self-Motivation
- Willingness to learn and take direction
- Reliable
- Availability
- Team Player

Online versus personally turned in applications: Once you are clear on what you'd like to see from an employee, the challenge becomes how to assess these strengths during the application and interview process, *prior* to them being hired.

The assessment of these qualities begins when the application is submitted. In today's world many employees have at least the option for applications to be submitted electronically. This will gain you more applicants because teens and young adults live in an online world.

However if applications are submitted in person, many of these qualities can be assessed at that time. Courtesy, communication and people skills, neatness and their grooming are a few that will be readily evident.

ASSESSING APPLICATIONS

Particularly when you are receiving an abundant number of applications, far more than positions available, assessing the applications is a necessary first step when it comes to hiring the best of today's teens and young adults.

You cannot simply interview applicants based on a "first in, first interviewed" strategy. It is an inefficient use of time, and more importantly may have you filling positions with less qualified employees. The superstars may have been buried in that stack of applications, and you never even talked with them.

Identifying your red and green flags:

The very first step in the process of assessing applications is to identify those measurable items that are important to you, and are in insight to an individuals likelihood of success. Those are the "green" flags. Put them in the stack of to be interviewed.

The absence of these items, or the wrong answers, are your "red" flags. Put them in the stack of do not interview. Based on your application flow, there may be times when you'll need to take a second look at these, so be sure to keep on file.

> Red means stop and green means go,
> when it comes to interviewing applications.

Examples of red and green flags;

Job History: With a young workforce, often times you are hiring individuals for their first job. However, if already having a job and experience in the workplace is important to you, then this should be a flag for you to consider. Don't overlook volunteering activities, yard work, school duties, and extra curricular examples as a reflection of job history.

Availability: Your business needs employees to be available when you need them. Even if you offer flexible scheduling, the more restrictive an applicants availability is should be considered now. Even the best of employees lose value if they can't work when you need them.

Handwriting and Spelling: If you require that employees be able to write communications and notes for their coworkers and supervisors, then hand-writing and spelling should be considered. Additionally, the neatness and legibility of their writing may be an indicator of their organization skills.

Completeness: Applications from your most qualified candidates will be submitted fully completed. Nothing will be left blank. You can use the flag system to separate these applicants.

Letters of Recommendation: What other employers or adults in the lives of a teen have to say about their past performance should be an indicator of future performance. And if the teen has taken the time to collect and submit these letters of recommendation, it demonstrates real initiative on their part. A definite green flag!

Timeliness: If your communication was clear as to when applications should be submitted, then you can use that as a flag. It may be an indicator of how well they'll follow guidelines if they were employees.

Personal follow up: A measurement of initiative, interest and a willingness to learn can be assessed through personal follow up that an applicant demonstrates.

Career interest: If an applicant has an interest in, and/or is currently studying the profession, industry or career that your position falls within, then consider this a green flag.

Current employee referral: Based on the performance of the employee doing the referring, you can decide if this should be a red or green flag. A teenage employee will generally send you someone just like themselves. But you may want to simply give this a green flag as a courtesy to your employees. If you have an internal recruitment program, then this should be a strong green flag.

It's will be up to you to decide which of these are given a higher priority and have the biggest impact on your business. At different times you may require all of your flag items to be green to move forward, but at other times it may be necessary to move applications forward with a less number of green flags.

Key Point: Be sure your applications are set up to ask the questions that will provide you with the answers necessary to determine if they will be placed in the red or green category.

THE PRE-INTERVIEW

After you have assessed the applications, you are in a position to schedule interviews. Prior to meeting with the applicant is the pre-interview period. This is a time for you to garner some additional information and insights from the applicant prior to the interview.

Following are guidelines for the pre-interview period;

Schedule enough time: Don't be rushed during this period or for the interview. Provide at least 30 minutes, maybe more. If you are attempting to move too many people through the process too quickly, you will not end up hiring the best of today's teens and young adults.

Be sure applicant is welcomed and made to feel comfortable: Whomever you have greeting the applicant is a key part of the success equation. That may be someone different than you, and they will be interacting with the applicant. The first thing is to simply have them welcome the applicant and make them feel comfortable. Besides being the hospitable thing to do, you don't want a young person to be nervous during the interview. You want them to feel at ease to freely answer questions in their natural style. How they are greeted and welcomed can greatly influence that.

● ●

*It's not just the interviewer
who effects hiring. All current
employees can play a role.*

● ●

Have them write something: In a day an age of online applications, you may not have had the opportunity to assess writing skills, spelling and legibility. Those may be important for you to know, and could be a deciding factor between applicants. There are some suggestions noted below but it could be as simple as completing or rewriting a part of the application.

Have applicants take test: There are a variety of tests you can have an applicant take. It could be a basic math test to determine if they can give back change. Or a test with questions that attempts to identify certain character traits. You want this done prior to the interview, and this is a perfect time to start.

Have applicant write answers to specific questions: There are a variety of questions that you can ask that will yield answers that can be very revealing about future performance. These answers can also help to be deciding factors between applicants getting hired. Asking 3 – 6 questions is plenty. This also can serve as the guideline for having them write something that is noted above.

Following are some examples of questions you can consider. Be creative though, you may be able to come up with better questions that are more specific to your needs on your own;

- What appeals to you about working at our company?

- Tell me about the last time you missed or were significantly late for work? What was the outcome?

- Tell me about the last time when you had to follow a dress code at work or school? Did you follow this on a consistent basis?

- Give me an example of a time you had to deal with a very frustrating or stressful situation at work?

- Describe a time when you failed to meet a customer expectation? What happened? What was the outcome?

- Tell me about a time you received critical feedback on your performance. How did you react to the feedback?

*Do the applicant's answers
demonstrate personal responsibility
or do they blame others?*

Review application, tests and answered questions: Prior to the interview, be sure you have adequate time to review the application, and any tests or questions that were issued during the pre-interview. The interviewer needs to be already familiar with the applicant prior to meeting with them.

INTERVIEW ENVIRONMENT
A big mistake we have seen played out often is that the interview is rushed. A very busy manager is also the person who interviews. They look at an application, look at the appli-

cant, ask a few questions without really letting the applicant answer, and say… "when can you start?" This same manager is always the person who complains about the quality of their workforce and how much time they have to spend interviewing.

Don't let this be you. Invest in this time interviewing prospective new employees. If done well, it will pay huge dividends.

The following guidelines will assist you in this process;

Quiet with minimum of interruptions: Do not interview on the shop floor, in the dining room or while you are still taking calls and answering questions for others. Focus on the interview and the applicant sitting in front of you. Do everything you can to clear your schedule so that interviewing is a priority.

* *

Do everything you can to clear your schedule so that interviewing is a priority

* *

Provide the applicant with the who, what, where, when, why and how of your company: Teens and young adults need to know the background and the purpose behind everything they do. Even though they applied with your company, don't assume they know about you. Tell them what your organization does and what is expected from an employee. The hours they will be expected to work, the types of jobs they will perform and the levels of service they must provide. This should be the majority of talking you should do in the interview. The applicant may take themselves out of contention when they realize they will have to work every Saturday night... and that would be a good thing!

Be prepared: Prior to meeting with the applicant, be sure you have familiarized yourself with them. Review the application, and any tests and questions prior to the interview. This should take just a few minutes, but gives you the insight of some key questions you can ask.

Ask open-ended questions. Let them do the talking. Through the submitted application, noted observational comments, tests and completed questions, you probably know if you want to hire this person or not. The interview ought to be a time for them to demonstrate their abilities to communicate, maturity, composure, eye contact and smiles. Everything that is hard, if not impossible, to capture prior to this moment. Ask them relevant questions about your expectations, or follow-ups and clarifications to what they have already turned in.

. . . .
During the interview, let them do the talking
. . . .

Take notes during the interview: While they are doing the talking, feel free to make a note of anything that jumps out to you, positive or negative about the applicant. It's easy to forget meaningful observations after the interview. And it may be this information that effects their rating and who you hire. Are they making eye contact with you and smiling, and how did they dress for the interview are two basic observations that often get overlooked. Don't be surprised if someone is not smiling at your customers, and is always being counseled on your grooming standards, if they aren't representing this during the interview.

Immediately after interview, review notes and rate applicant: Do not interview five to ten people and then sit back and make your notes. Too much will blend together. Spend the necessary time, maybe five minutes, just after the interview to note any comments and observations you have, and then to complete a rating sheet.

Rating applicant: Completing a quantifiable rating guide is critical when it comes to hiring the best. It sets you and your prospective new employee up for success. Rate on the areas that are the most important to you and your businesses success. Set a minimum hiring score and only offer positions to those who have exceeded that level. This system is flexible enough to allow you to change your hiring score based on the incoming flow of qualified applicants. Additionally, it will identify areas of strength and those that require improvement. This is very beneficial in making the training process productive.

Note: If you'd like an example of a rating guide, go to; www. WAVESforSuccess.com.

Pre-employment testing: One additional process you could undertake prior to offering the applicant a job is to have additional employment testing completed. There are professional companies that can provide you with testing mechanisms that are scientifically valid, and will paint a fairly accurate picture of dependability, honesty and integrity of a person. Drug testing may even be a requirement. It is something that you may want to consider. They come with an expense, and we could provide you with names of companies that provide that service.

For most hourly, entry level, seasonal jobs that are filled with high school and college students, this additional level of testing can be expensive and not necessary. The process that has already been addressed will provide you with enough background and insight to make very educated decisions on hiring the best of today's teens and young adults.

ORIENTATION & TRAINING GUIDELINES

Now that you have identified the perfect candidates, assessed your applications, garnered additional information through tests and questions, and productively interviewed, you have put yourself in a position to hire the best of today's teens and young adults!

To fully leverage the abilities and contributions of this age group, the initial training and orientation is a key piece.

While this chapter is not about training, following are guidelines that will get your initial training off to a successful start. This is a critical period for a new hire in how they engage with your company, and greatly influences their retention and contributions.

Use computer and video training: This is an age group that has been raised with computers and video. It is how they are "wired" to learn and retain information. Invest in, or create, computer based training. When combined with the impact of a dynamic trainer, your new hires will quickly contribute in meaningful ways.

Create video message for all new hires to watch: A dynamic trainer is critical in your training process. But there are certain messages that should be repeated, that can be delivered in a more effective way. Creating a video message that talks about your expectations, purpose, mission and values will get "heard" better in this form than in person. Maybe your founder, or president is the one on screen. Producing a short, highly impactful, age appropriate video is inexpensive and will always deliver results.

Invest in initial training: Many companies fall short here. They do everything else well, and then when it comes to training they simply send their new hires into action. Accurate information is soon lost and bad habits are quickly acquired. Take a fresh look at the amount of time, budget and the level of quality of your initial training.

Only have policies that are relevant and able to be consistently enforced: Take a fresh look at your policies, processes and procedures. If you have guidelines that are not able to be enforced or are outdated, get rid of them. Whatever is actually occurring is the new policy anyway.

Use this as an opportunity to focus on what the most important policies are that effect customer service, safety and your businesses success, and then demand 100% compliance in those areas.

> The more unnecessary rules you have
> can tend to take your managers eyes
> off of your core business.

Romance history of company and community participation: Teens want to be a part of something bigger than themselves. Share with them the history of your company and your role in the community. Many will find this fascinating information and build a bridge of loyalty and increased participation and willingness to learn. This should be built into a video message that was described above.

Have a process that determines when initial training is successfully completed: Just because someone has "done the time" does not mean that they are ready to be on their own. Have tests in place, and a manager who is responsible for this final piece of the initial training.

If you want your employees to not only retain all of the information you have given them, but more importantly to adopt this information while at work, then give them the reasons behind every policy. This is an age group that asks a lot of questions. That won't simply take things on face value and because you have told them to. They want to know the background and purpose behind a policy or procedure. Just because it is logical to you, do not assume it makes any sense to them or that they understand its necessity.

. . . .

**Don't just train on "What" the policy
or procedure is, but also test on
"Why" the policy is in place.**

. . . .

A final note: All information that you use in your initial training and orientation should be replicated on an employee website. Let them review your company history, values, policies, procedures and videos when it is convenient for them.

CHAPTER 13

Make It a Mission...
Not a Job

As I write the final chapter of this book I'm left with just a few observations and final thoughts.

What I've seen is that most employers of teens are committed to the success of their employees and their communities. They want what is best for both.

Businesses support teens' commitments, school and extra curricular activities. Accommodations are made to insure that academic and family pursuits take precedence over work priorities. Life advice is offered, and typically there is some type of program that offers prizes and rewards for a job well done.

In part, those are all elements of WAVES and ought to suggest that they have a handle on how to manage teens.

So why do so many businesses struggle with, and remain frustrated over, how to recruit, retain and motivate teenagers at work?

I have three beliefs about this:

SPEED OF CHANGE AND THE SPEED OF LIFE

I believe that the first factor is it's the *speed of change and the speed of life* that is occurring in our culture. Technology, information, entertainment and communication are all instantly available, and evolve on nearly a daily basis. Teens' entire lives have been shaped by this pace and they are early adopters to all technological advances.

SOCIETAL CHANGES

Society has changed over the last generation and its face continues to look different. Today's teens are exposed to a different environment than what impacted others not much older than they are. Family structure and involvement is different. Too much structure collides with increasing unsupervised time. Schools don't provide the spectrum of programs, campus violence is top of mind daily, and academics have suffered. Today's heroes and role models tend to reflect sports and celebrity instant millionaires that don't necessarily promote values and personal responsibility.

LACK OF UNDERSTANDING BY OWNERS, MANAGERS, SUPERVISORS

The pace of change is so swift that *business owners, managers and supervisors just don't understand* what's different or even willing to acknowledge that there is a difference. They continue to manage through the eyes of when they were teens, not through the eyes of a teenager today. It's a big difference, leaving employers working harder with fewer results.

I believe that the reason there continues to be high levels of angst regarding teens, is because while most business people mean well, they execute incorrectly. It's simply hard to keep up.

The irony is that even though teenagers can generate frustration and confusion at work, teens are the solution! This age group has the ability to contribute at levels not available to any group prior.

The missing ingredient is practical workplace readiness. That has fallen off the "how to develop a teen to be a contributing adult" list. If that skill is added to their base of knowledge and information access, along with adjusting your communications and motivating techniques to a more age-appropriate level, you'll see amazing results.

Today's teens are phenomenal and are ready to be motivated and inspired at work. Employers have a tremendous opportunity and unintended community responsibility to have an even bigger influence in their lives.

It doesn't matter if your teen employee is Stanford bound or struggling to get through high school. I believe the role of employers of youth has changed. Elements of what used to be taught at home, schools or church are now becoming the responsibility of employers. That is only if you accept it.

Your motivations may vary. You can do it because you care about the youth in your community, it makes your job easier when your shifts are filled, customer service, product quality and your bottom line will improve, or because you want to make a lasting impact on those people you come in close contact with.

Employers can't perform miracles, though. I haven't spent any time focusing on those teens who aren't ready for the workforce except to say you should remove them from your team. A lot can be said about the benefits of hiring the right person. There are plenty of teens that aren't a good match for the position you have available. They don't have the maturity or frame of mind to be employed. Pre-applicant screening and effective interviewing skills will give you teens with a predisposition and willingness to be motivated at work.

Your Challenge:

To Be Effective... Not Just Efficient

Go beyond the handbook, policies, procedures and rules. Don't feel good about yourself because you've checked all the boxes and thoroughly completed all legal documents.

Get to know your employees. Know their interests, goals, hobbies, and concerns. Ask for their feedback and suggestions.

Adjust Your Reality to Theirs

A teen's life environment has been altered. They do not see life the same way as a person that is just a few years, or a generation older.

Understand teens and manage their workplace performance through their eyes, not through the lens of when you were a teen.

MAKE IT A MISSION. NOT A JOB

View the role as an employer bigger than it is. Show up each day utilizing your influence and educating your teens. Look at the big picture of where they want to be five years from now, and help them get there.

Enjoy the journey. Don't expect that the inclusion of one new strategy will make permanent radical improvements. There will continue to be ups and downs, but with the WAVES approach the tide will rise.

Employing teens just got easier. I hope the information in this book has informed and enlightened at a level to provide you a fresh perspective and approach to managing teens.

I look forward to hearing of the challenges you have faced, and the successes you have experienced.

The best is yet to come.

Resources

The following pages have additional tips, strategies, techniques and lists of information designed to improve recruitment, education, motivation, hiring or retention of a young adult workforce.

This information should be downloadable from our website, or email us to receive copies. We will continue to post free value-added information for your use.

Visit us at www.wavesforsuccess.com for updated free information.

a. 8 Reasons Why Teens Quit

b. 10 Retention Tips

c. Recruiting Ideas for *Today's* Teens

d. The 8 'C's for Teenage Prizes and Incentives

e. Bill Gate's Quotes

f. 101 Ways to Recruit, Educate, Retain and Motivate Today's Teens

8 Reasons Why Teens Quit

1. Lack of Recognition
   Recognition equals retention. If you ignore their contributions and milestones... they'll be gone.

2. Promises Not Kept
   What was presented at the interview is not reality. Flexible schedules, job duties, advancements and other benefits never happen.

3. No Follow Up
   When managers/supervisors of teens say they will follow up... they better follow up.

4. Job Assignments
   Always stuck doing the same task or always given the job duties no one likes to do.

5. Bored
   Mix it up a little. Teens get bored easily. Cross train and regularly allow for change in work duties.

6. Coworkers
   If you allow non-performing teens to continue working, your quality teens will hit the door.

7. No Respect
   Today's teens want their input and performance to matter. Ignore them or give them the perception that they don't matter, and they'll be gone.

8. Substantially More Pay
   If the work environment is right, teens won't quit for the opportunity to earn a small raise.

1 0 Retention Tips

1. Recognition: *Recognition equals retention. The more you focus on catching people doing something right, and highlighting their successes and milestones at work, and away from work, the longer they will stay.*

2. Incentive Pay: *Don't just give another 25¢ raise. Create a win-win scenario, and pay a bonus on specific menu items, products or services that you sell.*

3. Instant Gratification: *Prizes, bonuses or other types of incentives need to be issued quickly. Daily is great. Monthly is far too long.*

4. Workplace Environment: *Work areas should be colorful and occasionally change. Where appropriate, have a place where pictures can be displayed and music played. Be a feel good, fun environment.*

5. Supervisor/Manager: *A caring supervisor/manager can do more for retention that just about anything else.*

6. Flexible Scheduling: *Be willing to allow your teen employee to participate in extra curricular activities and attend significant personal events. You can become the employer of choice!*

7. Include in Decision Making Process: *Whether you ask them one at a time, or have an employee suggestion program, soliciting your current teen employees input will make them fiercely loyal.*

8   Promote Quickly: *If your teen is a superstar performer, promote them into a more responsible position quickly. At least find other responsibilities that they can own. If not, they'll find an employer that challenges them more.*

9. Provide Respect: *Loyalty can be built on your respect of your teen employees. Verbally let them know that you appreciate their contributions.*

10. Co-workers: *If you apply all of these retention builders you will have built an attractive team of co-workers. Teens will love this and stay.*

Recruiting Ideas for *Today's* Teens

Place employment ads on the Internet: Purchase banner ads on websites that current employees frequent. It is likely other teens are also on those sites.

Use employment websites: Like snagajob.com, gotajob. com, teens4hire.org, craigslist.org. Cast a wide net and be in many places.

Develop a profile on Facebook.com: Ask current employees to add your company to their friend network. This will make your company visible to everyone in your employee's social network.

Be very visible at schools: Postings should be engaging, with age appropriate design and humor to communicating your employment message. Simple "Help Wanted" and "Now Hiring" signs do not attract attention.

Create strategic retail partners: Work hard to find other businesses (where teens shop and/or hang out) that you can build a partnership with to communicate your employment opportunities. Purchase your incentives from the businesses, give them free product or passes. By aligning yourself with select music and clothing stores, restaurants and movie theatres, you will put the company name in front of prospective teen staff.

Direct all prospective applicants to an easily remembered web site address: All new teen staff should apply online at your website.

Provide services to schools: Do not just be an employer. Get involved with curriculum development and volunteer services by training in business, economics and work experience classes. Get involved. You will build trust with the teenagers ahead of time.

Loyal customers can make loyal employees: Where appropriate, communicate to your customers that you have positions available and the benefits they would receive by being a part of the team. Also, share this message with your season pass holders, membership groups or those who receive your company newsletter.

Do not make prospective employees wait: Acknowledge all applications within 24-48 hours with a quick phone call or email. Thank them for applying, let them know you are reviewing the application and will contact them if an interview needs to be scheduled.

Use your current teen staff as recruiters: Quicker loyalty can be built with a peer. On school visits and at job fairs be sure to include young staff members as recruiters. Let them tell their story.

Use TV advertising: Create specific ads for television geared to your jobs. Run on local channels. Do NOT expect results from classified ads in newspapers.

Internal recruitment program: Have a program in place that motivates through money, rewards, or both, to your current staff to recruit as many people as possible. Do not penalize them for success – give them a challenge and let them go for it!

Offer a signing bonus: Pay a new employee to begin working with you. Use this as a "Limited Time Offer." Make sure the new employee has to work a certain amount of hours prior to receiving the signing bonus. The bonus does not have to be much nor does it have to even be cash.

The 8 'C's for Teenage Prizes and Incentives

1. Cars (Gas/Washes)
2. Clothes
3. Concerts
4. CD's
5. Certificates/Cards
6. Cinema
7. Cash
8. Customize any of the above

The following was quoted from part of a speech given by Bill Gates, Microsoft Chairman, to Whitney High School students.

Circa early 2000

Rule 1:   Life is not fair – get used to it.

Rule 2:   The world won't care about your self-esteem. The world will EXPECT you to accomplish something BEFORE you feel good about yourself.

Rule 3:   You will NOT make $40,000 a year right out of high school. You won't be a vice-president with a car phone until you earn both.

Rule 4:   If you think your teacher is tough, wait until you meet your boss.

Rule 5:   Flipping burgers is not beneath your dignity. Your grandparents had a different word for burger flipping – they called it opportunity.

Rule 6:   If you mess up it's not your parents' fault, so don't whine about your mistakes, learn for them.

Rule 7:   Before you were born, your parents weren't as boring as they are now. They got that way from paying your bills, doing your laundry and listening to you talk about how cool you are. So before you save the rain forest from the parasites of your parents' generation, try delousing the closet in your own room.

Rule 8:   Your school may have done away with winners and losers, but life has not. In some schools, they have abolished failing grades and they'll give you as many times as you want to get the right answer. This doesn't bear the slightest resemblance to ANYTHING in real life.

Rule 9:   Life is not divided into semesters. You don't get the summers off and very few employers are interested in helping you find yourself. Do that on your own time!

Rule 10: Television is NOT real life. In real life people actually have to leave the coffee shop and go to jobs.

Rule 11: Be nice to nerds. Chances are you'll end up working for one.

101 Ways to Recruit. Educate. Retain and Motivate Today's Teens

RECRUITING

1. Don't jump to conclusions
2. Do not always think you are right
3. Train your mind to focus
4. Get the details
5. Use open-ended questions
6. Use descriptive praise
7. Utilize web-collaboration
8. Look for dependability
9. Give sincere compliments on the positive things you've seen
10. Introduce new employees to others employees within the first few days
11. Have clear organizational policies
12. Be flexible
13. Be patient
14. Hire their friends
15. Look for leaders
16. Hire the best
17. Try to see teens as equals and forget about age
18. Teens place a high value on self fulfillment
19. Support the technology teens use in their personal lives
20. Commit to socially responsible causes
21. Understand teens personal strengths and limitations
22. Participate in community events
23. Listen to pros & cons from current employees
24. Have clear job responsibility

25. Understand teens are very competitive
26. Don't judge

MOTIVATING

27. Have respect for teen's ideas
28. Spend one-on-one time
29. Let them bring out the kid in you
30. Cultivate a sense of humor
31. Send company-wide emails that recognize an employee's success
32. Give teens a cause
33. Have training initiatives
34. Keep employees engaged
35. Treat all teens fairly
36. Have helpful supervisors
37. Create opportunities to learn new skills/ advancement
38. Don't have a judgmental attitude
39. Have fun at work
40. Maintain eye contact or else your employees can lose their enthusiasm
41. Implement recognition and/or reward
42. Take the employees to lunch and then give them the rest of the afternoon off
43. Encourage employees to think for themselves
44. Offer referral bonuses
45. Be aware of peer pressure from other teens
46. Learn to read nonverbal clues
47. Appreciate them
48. Stick to your words
49. Keep teens informed on latest developments

RETAINING
50. Give a sense of entitlement
51. Know their psychological needs
52. Show care and concern
53. Treat teens as equals
54. Make them feel they are an important part of the team
55. Watch your tone of voice so that it is not demeaning
56. Admit mistakes
57. Follow through on your commitments
58. Model reliability
59. Monitor and evaluate the effectiveness of your retention program
60. Respect their schedule needs
61. Be honest
62. Do not try to manipulate teens
63. Build employee's self confidence
64. Appreciate them
65. Think beyond the short term
66. Talk with them
67. Be positive
68. Have an open-door policy
69. Trust goes both ways
70. Remove barriers to success
71. Listen to your team
72. Communicate effectively
73. Respect your team
74. Create a learning culture
75. Pick your battles
76. Respect their privacy
77. Grow with them

EDUCATING

78. Help teens see education as an investment
79. Work is not the most important thing in life
80. Learn their language
81. Give teens the benefit of the doubt
82. Walk in their shoes
83. Apply policies and rules consistently
84. Sometimes compromise is necessary
85. Contribute to a charity or cause in the employee's name
86. Identify variables leading to turnover
87. Foster a learning environment
88. If you're the boss, be the first one in
89. Moods and attitudes are contagious
90. Plant seeds, pull weeds
91. Consider different geographies
92. Do more than expected, never less
93. Always do the right thing
94. Delegate – Don't abdicate
95. Lead – Don't manage
96. Set clear goals
97. Learn to text message
98. Continue to show you are competent & empowered
99. The first few minutes of the workday can be the most important
100. Define employee engagement
101. Pay attention to language

About the Author
Ken Whiting

A common thread throughout Ken's business background has been as an employer of teenagers and young adults. Through his business interests he has been directly responsible for the hiring, training and motivating of over 5,000 high school and college age employees.

From that experience, combined with feedback from many other teenage labor-intensive employers, he created the *WAVES for Success* system for improving workplace performance. He continues to focus on ways of understanding, in today's culture, what inspires them to participate, contribute and excel at work. Through his success with WAVES, he lectures regularly on the subjects of Teenage Workforce and Supervisory Success, to organizations and businesses that employ and develop youth.

In 2008 his *WAVES for Teenage Workforce Success* book was published, and from its launch has been met with rave reviews on content and insight. Additionally his articles have appeared in over one hundred magazines and newspapers, securing his reputation as the nations foremost expert on providing solutions to teenage and young adult workforce challenges.

He has sat on boards and committees for many local, state, national and international industry associations. He is a past president of both the Santa Cruz Area Chamber of Commerce and Rotary Clubs, and been a volunteer with many charitable, church and civic organizations.

Married to Renee for 30 years, they have three daughters and reside in Surf City... Santa Cruz, California.

• Keynote Presentations
• Seminar Leader
• Consulting

Contact Ken today
Ken@wavesforsuccess.com